MW01140916

COLLECTION OF POEMS

AND WRITINGS

Faith, Family, Friends

BY BILL SWAIN

Bill Swain

Compiled 2015

Order someone a copy today from
CreateSpace estore or Amazon.com

FORWARD

In his 87 years of life, our father has written many poems, but has never chosen to have them published. However, he has printed and given away many, many thousands of them. So, for this Christmas of 2015, we, his children, are giving him a big SURPRISE by having a large portion of his poems printed, including a picture of the Scroll of the entire Bible he has written on one continuous, unspliced scroll, and the music to one of his songs. Also, he has written some history of his life, which he intended to be only for his family; but, we are including it in this book hoping it will help you better understand more about him and why he chooses to put so much of his thoughts in poems and writings.

Children: Terri Miller, Ginger Roberts, William "Bill" Swain

CONTENTS

FAMILY

FRIENDS

Things I Remember about Myself
By Bill Swain

Here are some of the things I remember from my early childhood, from 2 years old and up; a little history about myself and where I grew up, and some other important (some maybe not so important) things I knew about and/or experienced in life. I was born in Scotland, Arkansas on May 22, 1928 to Opal Vesta O'Neal Swain and William Theodore Swain. My father died when I was 5 months old and was buried on my mother's 18th birthday, November 5th, 1928. He was 26 years old.

When I was 7 months old, Mother and I then came to Bowlegs, Oklahoma to live with her parents William Robert O'Neal and wife Ada Dell Casinger O'Neal. The BIG OIL BOOM was in "FULL BLAST"!!! Bowlegs was located in the center of the OIL BOOM which was located in the center of the old Indian Nation which became Seminole County when Oklahoma became a state in 1907. When oil was struck (discovered) all kinds of people rushed in like they did when gold was struck in California … and it was GOLD! Black GOLD!!! Several oil wells produced 10,000 barrels a day and I know of 1 that produced over 13,000 barrels a day. But many of the people who rushed in were after the "fast dollar" and the wide open, illegal and wicked ways of life. Understand the state was only 20 years old when the OIL BOOM really exploded in intensity in 1927 and 1928.

There were hardly any roads. Most of the roads were just old cow and wagon trails, and when it rained very much, they were impassable. 1927 and 1928 were two of the heaviest rain years we have had. There were very few

10

organized cities or towns, police systems, housing or means or organized ways of taking care of the people who swarmed into this territory like they did during the gold rush in California. People "lived" everywhere. In tents, makeshift houses, some in their cars etc. Some camped out.

Back then the car tags were numbered according to the population of each county. Oklahoma County was #1-xxxx, Tulsa County #2-xxxx, and Seminole County#3-xxxx. The towns were wide open, similar to the "old wild west days"! The Oklahoma City newspaper, THE DAILY OKLAHOMAN, sent reporters to Seminole County for over a week to visit various towns to observe and report on the lawlessness, crime and prostitution going on there. These reports and stories were carried on the front page of the DAILY OKLAHOMAN every day for an 8-day period from Oct. 4 to Oct. 11, 1928. On October 4, 1928 the headlines read, VICE RING RULES SEMINOLE COUNTY. Sub paragraphs say, Where Is The Law, and Law Winks At Gambling And Prostitution. The sheriff had painted a big white line across the northern end of the main street and promised not to bother the people if they stayed on the other side of the line. This "wild area" of Seminole was called BISHOPS ALLEY. This is where I grew up during my early childhood days (pre teen days).

There were no restrictions on how many wells you could drill or how much oil you could produce. The largest gasoline refinery in the world was less than 3 miles from Bowlegs. At one time there were 27 gasoline refineries within a 5 or 6 mile radius of Seminole and this area produced 1/5th of the gas and oil in the US. Five of these refineries burned down and my wife Dixie lived in the closest house to the Sinclair Gasoline Plant # 12 when it exploded and burned in 1941. She was separated from her family and thought they had been burned up. There were 27 gasoline storage tanks at this refinery that exploded, one by one, and each time the gasoline was thrown up and the whole sky was on fire. She ran and ran crying and screaming. One of her friends came by and tried to get her in a car, but every time he got near another tank would explode and the fire would fly overhead and she would run away. Finally, he did get her into the car and they found that her parents were safe. That young boy who picked her up was Don Dixon. He later invented the first zero turning radius lawn mower and he had his company in Houston, Texas.

There were also areas of large metal tanks ranging in size from 30,000, to 50,000 and some 80,000 barrel-tanks (THIS MEANS BARRELS, NOT GALLONS) to store the oil in until it could be used locally, or hauled away. There might be 10, 20, 30, 40 or even 50 of these tanks built close together in an area called a tank farm. At this time the Seminole railroad handled more freight than the Chicago rail yard. One day in 1927 it handled 24,015 rail cars, and back then the railroad ran even to Bowlegs. A special railroad called the "Wewoka Switch" which ran from Seminole to Wewoka had to be built to handle all of the rail business. During this time many oil wells were drilled so close that one leg of two different wells rested on the same foundation and you may look out and see from 50 to 100 hundred wells, or more if you happened to be in the right place. Every oil well drilled had a large derrick that stood from 60 to 120 feet in the sky and when they were lighted and at night the landscape looked similar to a large city. Each oil well engine made a great big "chug chug sound." There was so much oil produced then that the price of oil dropped to 15 cents a barrel and the governor stopped all drilling and production until the price rose to $1.00 a barrel which took about a year. And remember, this was about the time the great depression began to take place. When all of the oil business was shut down and soon after the depression hit most of the "undesirables, the crooks, outlaws, prostitutes and people who were after quick money, etc" moved on and left mostly good people. Bowlegs became a poor town, but a quiet town and a great place to live after the BOOM! Pretty Boy Floyd who robbed his first bank in Earlsboro, which Dixie's best friend's father owned, had been killed.   The bank-robbing Kimes brothers had also been caught and the undesirables moved out.

There were then three churches, Baptist, Methodist and Pentecostal in Bowlegs. (Three of the Baptist pastors at Bowlegs later became three of the leading pastors in the Baptist Convention. T.B. Lackey became head of the Convention and the Lackey Manor rest home in Okla. City is named after him. Judson Cook became head of the Boys Ranch Town and A.L. Lowther, who grew up in Scotland, Ark. and was a friend of the family there, became one of the leading evangelists. Jake Self who later was a pastor at Bowlegs was killed in the big Tornado that killed about 50 people in Okla. City.). Back then Oklahoma was a dry state, alcohol was illegal, there were no casinos and only one beer joint in Bowlegs which didn't last long. "For some reason????" many of the beer joints burned down, usually around 2 or 3 o'clock in the morning.

Businesses closed on Sundays. Teachers could whip their students and parents could whip their kids. One day, Mother gave me 8 whippings. I didn't like it at the time but now I don't regret them. I had heard the word "gay" but that was another word for happy! I never heard the word "lesbian" until I was grown and married. All of the couples

13

that I knew who were living together were married and although there may have been some baby born out of wedlock I didn't know of any during my school days. (I won't repeat what the Bible calls these mothers, fathers and babies.) I was proud to be an "Okie" back then....but now????????????

When the oil business was allowed to resume, many regulations were put into effect, and drilling and production were greatly limited. The oil business and the communities and towns became a much more "settled" business. Bowlegs grew from not having a High School when the oil boom hit to becoming the largest Union Graded rural school in the United States. On Sunday, August 29, 1934 the Daily Oklahoman carried the story and a picture of the school and student body on their front page.

Things I remember:
age 2… I was so cute (ha ha) the neighbor lady dressed me up in a dress..... I remember seeing someone's shoe thrown in a pond others trying to get it out.
age 2 or 3… our house being moved to another location..... Falling into a big ditch which we called the deep-hole and crawling back up the steep bank by holding onto tree roots. I was mad, and crying because my folks didn't hear me calling.

age 4… going 6 miles from Bowlegs to Maud, and back, in a wagon.

age 5… Grandad building us a new house..... Our dog having pups under our house..... My granddad drove a school bus and kept it parked in a garage at our house. One day I crawled on top of the bus when it was parked in the garage and fell off, head first, between the bus and side of the garage. My head hit the bottom frame of the side of the garage and split my head open pretty bad. We were in the midst of flooding conditions and on the way to the doctor's office I remember seeing chickens roosting on top of a stove, surrounded by flood waters, that someone had set out in their yard.... I remember when Highway 99 was opened up and paved from Seminole to Ada... I remember on a return trip from Arkansas, whoever took us to the railroad track out in the country where there was no train station, rolled up some newspapers and set them on fire and stood on the tracks waving them at the train. It stopped and picked us up.

age 6... going to school the first day.... Peeing on the floor in 1st grade. After that I didn't have to get permission to go to the bath room..... The famous WWII pilot, Jimmy Doolittle, brought his air show to Letha, Okla. and took people for rides and also dropped watermelons out of the planes similar to dropping bombs.....Walking to church on the muddy road and carrying our shoes until we got to the church.....The first picture show I ever saw was shown on the outside of Butch's grocery store in Bowlegs and it was a John Wayne movie.

age 7...2nd grade   a boy so big and fat he made us look like midgets.... The Ringling Brothers, Barnum and Bailey Circus came to Letha and erected their tents in and around the baseball field. I saw several rodeos and famous old time cowboys at the rodeos held in the base ball park, Tom Mix, Gene Autry etc. Dixie's aunt was married to Gene's cousin....... We went "noodling" for fish in the Washita River and caught about 300 pounds of catfish and buffalo. A big event for a 7-year-old boy!

age 8…3rd grade   My Granddad died. How much it hurt me..... I was at the hospital to see my Granddad when the ambulance brought in Chris Whitson, the deputy sheriff, who had just been murdered..... My granddad's father and mother, Robert Nicholson O'Neal and wife Nancy were living with us at that time. After his death they went back to Arkansas and lived with one of their other children.... One day in school I drew a picture in art class and the teacher didn't believe I drew it, she accused me of tracing it.

age 9…4th grade, We played marbles and spiked tops at recess.....We went to Wewoka Lake to watch 4th of July fireworks......One day after it had rained I was playing in the yard and a big ball of fire raced across the sky traveling from the east to the west. It was very spectacular. I don't know if I witnessed some historic event or not??? ...I accepted Jesus Christ as my personal Savior and was baptized at the First Baptist Church...... Some of my greatest memories in life happened at that Church. When I was 13 years old. I had a friend who never walked nor went to school a day in his life, and he could hardly speak but he had a good mind. One day in that church Leo Pool crawled, on his hands and knees, to accept Jesus Christ as his personal Savior. I wrote a poem about him (MY FRIEND). There was also a girl, Doris Graham, a sister of one of my classmates, who went to church there who was cripple and never went to school a day in her life. Mother invited her to her Sunday school class and she accepted Jesus as her savior.   Up until 2 years ago (2010) she had not missed one day of Sunday School in the last 54 years! She has perfect attendance medals hanging all over her wall. She is now in a rest home at Seminole.

age 10…5th grade,   One of my classmates, Vernon Proctor, stepped off of the school bus in front of a car and was killed

16

immediately....Our grade school softball team got to go to Wewoka to a ball tournament...... One of my girl classmates got married when she was 15 years old. Back then many people were so poor that getting an education was not so important and many families moved around so much that their children didn't go to school, and sometimes there wasn't even a school where they did live..... People used to come by our house and beg for clothing and food. Many children had to work to help the family survive and got very little education. It was not uncommon to see 20 year old students in high school.

Also back in those days hardly anyone had running water. We had to draw (pull) our water out of a deep well with a rope and that was pretty hard to do. So, on wash days after the washing and rinsing was over we would take our bath in the rinse water (whether we need one or not????? ha ha.) Back then I made most of my own toys: cars, bow and arrows, wagons, wheel bars, hoops and handle to push them along, tree houses, made swings and a log cabin and dug caves; and a little later, killed lots of squirrels and one year caught 16 squirrels for pets.

age 11...6th grade   One of my uncles took me to Wewoka to the county fair and on 4th of July took us to Wewoka lake to see fireworks......One day the teacher was going to spank a girl and she took the paddle away from the teacher and broke it. I never saw the girl again. She was 16.

age 12...7th grade   I remember well when WWII started, I know where I was when I heard the news. Porter heard it on his radio and came and told us...... In the seventh grade a classmate and neighbor to Vernon Proctor, Thomas McAllem crawled under his house and was electrocuted by a bare electric wire.... The 7th grade used 2 rooms separated by a boy's restroom and a girl's restroom. Each restroom had an access door from a hall that paralleled each restroom. Our homeroom teacher was a woman, Mrs. Snyder, and when she went from one room to the other she always went through the boy's hall. I never did figure out why??????

age 13…8th grade   One day in school our music teacher was absent and her husband, J.J. McCoy, the band teacher substituted for her. He had a "funny, or not so funny" way of conducting his class. You could talk and do a few other little things and get by with it, but when he got "his Fill" he exploded into rage!! So he got enough and exploded. He went up and down the isles slapping every boy on the jaws and yelling, "Have you had yours? Have you had yours?" Needless to say I got mine! We moved our house from west of Bowlegs to 1/2 mile east of Bowlegs and 1/4 mile south on a 40 acre farm that we owned. From that year on I farmed several of the acres with help from hired hands from time to time. When we used them we paid 15 cents an hour. Besides a garden with almost everything in it there is to plant, we raised head feed, corn, peanuts and thrashed and sold the peanuts to have a little money. Mamma, and mother helping at times when she wasn't working in Oklahoma City, canned about 400 quarts of vegetables each year. Sometimes we took vegetables, chickens etc. to Seminole and went door to door selling them. We raised chickens, hogs and had a cow, and two mules, which I used to plow with. I also had a horse. I butchered a hog or two each year that we cured for meat. I farmed every year until my Senior Year.

age 14…9th grade   I was the football mascot and Bowlegs had one of, if not the best, High School Football Teams in the State. There were only 2 classes of teams at that time, A and B Class. Bowlegs went undefeated in B Class that year and Seminole also went undefeated in A Class. They played each other and it ended in a 0 to 0 tie...... We didn't have running water or a bathtub so sometimes us guys would go to an oil well and (take a bath) go swimming in the warm water of the circulating tank. The circulating tank was a large tank about 12 or 15 feet across and 6 or 8 feet deep and was used to cool the water for the oil well engine that pumped the oil out of the ground. It had the same use as a car radiator is used today. Incidentally we didn't use a bathing suit. Back then the engines that pumped the oil out of the ground weren't small electric engines like today, they were large one-cylinder engine with the piston pumping parallel to the ground and they were 30 to 40 feet long and got very hot and had to have the water to cool them. They were gas engines and ran on the natural gas that came from the well.

Also back then most of the natural gas that came out of each oil well was discharged or burned. There were many gas torches that burned night and day just to burn up the gas. But, in the winter this gas would do like cold air reacts to a warm windowpane. Like the air turns into water, the natural gas would condense into gasoline. On some wells the companies would install a large pipe, called a "drip" where the gasoline condensed and collected. These drips would hold as much as 100 gallons of gasoline. Sometimes the companies picked up this gasoline and refined it, but usually they just let the gasoline run down a creek. My friend, that is where you could get FREE gasoline, DRIP GASOLINE as it was called. There was a 100-gallon drip by Dixie's house, but I never used it. The only thing, this gasoline had a strong odor and you could walk down the street and tell which cars were using drip. I'll bet some cars never had any other kind of gasoline in them in their life time!.....During summer months between 9th and 10th grades the school asked me to do some work there.

age 15...10th grade   During the war years, each class at school had a contest to see who could raise the most money to support the war effort. On Saturdays we gathered up scrap iron, brass and copper from the oil fields and anywhere else we could find it. We also gathered old auto tires and big 4 to 6 inch rubber hoses used in the oil fields to pump oil through. Rubber hoses were made out of real rubber then...... During the summer I went to Harvest in Kansas for a short time trying to make some money....After I returned I worked for Morgan Sash and Door in Oklahoma City, building doors and windows....At the end of the summer I told my fellow workers that I was leaving Friday and going back to school. They said they were leaving Friday and going back to Arkansas. I asked them where they were from and they said Scotland. I said I was born in Scotland, what's you name? They were my cousins, Filmore Hall and his son and I didn't even know them.... I thought about going to school in OKC but returned to Bowlegs.

age 16...11th grade, On Saturdays we continued gathering all kinds of scrape for the war effort...... I made the football team as quarterback and played every down of every game for our ten games. I played both offence and defense and called all of the signals. I remember that the quarterback for Okemah was also named Swain and we beat them. His brother is now married to Joan Strain (Frankie's sister)...I also made the basketball team. I worked for the school some during the summer and also worked some for Dresser Engineering repairing cooling towers for oil Companies. We had never owned a car, I had to walk or hitchhike everywhere I went. I'll bet I've hitchhiked 50 or more times between Bowlegs and Okla. City. Mother worked and lived most of the time during my high school days in Oklahoma City so I worked enough that summer to buy an old, no good 1936 Ford from one of my school friends who later was in charge of building the world famous Hubble Telescope. We are still good friends. I didn't keep the Ford but a few months and then decided to sell it. I thought I could just drive it to Oklahoma City, put a FOR SALE sign on it and some one would buy it. So I drove it to Oklahoma City, put a sign on it and parked it on Reno Ave.... and would you believe it, within an hour some guy came by and paid me in cash for it...and I was hitchhiking again, back to Bowlegs. Remember, during the war they didn't make cars and old cars were all you could get...Also almost everything was rationed, most foods, gasoline, etc.... I also helped build the house in Bowlegs that Dixie and I now live in. It was built for my uncle Claud O'Neal and wife Violet Kellogg. Years later Dixie and I had the house moved to Midwest City, and I must have remodeled it a "100" times. Incidentally my aunt Violet's mother was a Hyde before she married, and her grandparents owned Hyde Park in New York City, which later was owned by President Roosevelt.

age 17...12th grade   During the summer between my 11th and 12th grades we moved our house from the farm to Bowlegs, directly across from the High School Flag Pole and I remodeled part of the house into a School Cafe. The school had no cafeteria at that time. I built an extra room, built a bathroom and built counters, booths and seating and also built the kitchen and plumbed the water. This is the first time we ever had electricity, running water and a bathroom. We still did not have a phone, or car, but did get a radio. Of course there were no cell phones, no computers, no TV's, no spaceships, no air conditioners, no jets, no casinos, alcohol was illegal and highway patrols and

21

income tax had not long ago come into existence. That was so long ago that my World Book Encyclopedia said that if it were possible for an airplane to fly to the moon it would take 3 and 1/2 months.

I got my hand broken 2 days before the first football game and missed the first 2 games.... We won the district Championship in basketball. ...We played a real good BYNG team in the Regional Tournament and were leading them until late in the game and all of our senior player fouled out. We lost. For part of the school year I dated a girl, Margaret Mitchell, who later went by the professional name of Luke Bandle. She later managed the famous Kennedy Center in Washington, DC. Most of Pres. Nixon's cabinet members were on her board of directors. She ran the "Wolf Trap" entertainment Center across the river in Virginia and later was responsible for building Opera Houses in Los Angeles and Eugene, Oregon. Her son and husband were policemen, and both were murdered. She later died a pauper in the mid 2000's having lost all of their money in a Saudi Arabia oil venture.....The rest of the school year I dated Betty Jane Rice. She later married Darrell Abernathy and after serving in the Air Force several years, he retired, and organized, and was in charge of, the Air Transportation for the state of Wyoming until passing away. Betty still lives in Cheyenne.

age 18...college   I worked at odd jobs during the summer and enrolled at OBU for college. I didn't like college but made the first cut on OBU's basketball team. Bob Bass was on that team who later coached several pro teams. Also Guy Kerkindal was on that team and I later ran into him in Interlaken, Switzerland at a Christian Seminar. Since I didn't like college I quit OBU after the 1st semester and enrolled at Seminole Jr. College. I didn't like college there either but played on the basketball team and played against OU's B team in OU's old Field House (basketball court).

age 19... During the summer I built tables, booths, counters and benches for Fred Shell's new cafe in Bowlegs. I then enrolled again at Seminole Jr. College but didn't finish out the 1st semester. I was taking 4 subjects I hated, literature, Spanish, and some subjects in science and advanced math. So I quit. People told me that I would be sorry but I have never been sorry that I didn't get a College education. I believe that God has been very good to me and most of the jobs that I have had have come to me. I wasn't looking for them. I believe God sent them my way. I know it's different for different folks. Some jobs do require that you get a college education.

age 20... My Uncle Porter O'Neal worked for Continental Oil Co. and he said I could go to work for an oil field pump company in Oklahoma City named EMSCO Pump Co. which was part of Continental Supply Co. I moved to OKC that summer. I didn't have a car so I hitchhiked (or walked) everywhere I went. That fall I had just walked to the street to catch a ride and someone drove by me and turned on a street and motioned for me to come there but I didn't want to because I wanted to catch a ride to get to Bowlegs and the football game that night. But it turned out to be my friend and he was bringing me a brand new 1949 Chevy that mother had purchased for me in Seminole. I later made the payments, but I don't know how she got it, because during the war, and even after, everything was rationed and cars weren't built for several years. I hadn't had that new car but a week or two until someone arrived in the picture (DIXIE LEE YADON).

I am not trying to say that my life and lifestyle was "lily

white" but there were things I just would not do and places I would not go when I was growing up. I wouldn't drink, go to a dance, gamble, go anywhere I thought there might be trouble, or hang around anybody or anywhere I thought there might be trouble. I even thought about putting in a miniature golf range but I didn't want to influence people to just spend what little money they had on "fun." The Bible says in Isaiah 55: 2, Wherefore do you spend money for that which is not bread?   You see, I never had much money, and certainly not any to just "SPEND". I guess I was kinda' "tight" with what little I had and I didn't want to influence others to spend theirs either. I remember in the fifth grade one of my friends, Jack Code, got a 15-cent allowance a week, just to spend ever how he wanted to, and I thought that was one of the worst things I had ever heard of or seen to let a kid spend money like that!!!

And I didn't do other things in life because I didn't want to influence my children in the wrong way. Also I was real "choosy" in going with girls. If I heard or thought that a girl was kind of "wild" or might want to have sex, I wouldn't associate with them. Making the decision to get married, to find the right one, was very, very, very hard for me because to me marriage was for a lifetime. There could be no divorce! I wouldn't think of marrying a girl if I didn't think she believed basically like me. I wouldn't even consider marrying a girl if she attended a different denomination church that I did because I thought it might confuse the thinking of our future children.

Dixie was 16 and I was 20 when one Sunday I arrived from Oklahoma City at the First Baptist Church in a new 1949 Chevy. It wasn't long until we were dating. We dated for a little over a year, and after she finally decided between me and another fellow, we were married on Jan 27, 1950. She was 18 and I was 21. At that time, I was running a service station in Bowlegs. (I had come back to Bowlegs one day from Oklahoma City and Claud, who was running the Station at that time, told me he wanted me to run the station because he had another job he could take so I took over the station and ran it about a year... didn't make hardly any money). When we decided to get married I built another room onto the Cafe for us to live in. After running the station for about a year one day a fellow came by and wanted to run the station, so I sold him the inventory, which wasn't very much. A few days later the father of one of my schoolmates who was a Foreman for Dresser Engineering Co. came by and wanted me to go to Texas and go to work for them as a carpenter. So we put everything we owned in the back of the Chevy Coupe and went to Sanford, Texas. It was late fall of 1950 and soon the weather was extremely cold that winter. I carpentered outside every day but one that winter, even in zero degree temps. We missed one day of 10-degree weather, but the wind was blowing so hard you could hardly stand up and the chill factor was well below zero. We were building or adding to gasoline plants and refineries.

Our little 13-foot trailer that we rented had no bathroom, we had to "make a run" to another building. The trailer was so small that the bed touched the walls on three sides and at night our covers froze to the walls where the walls had sweated during the day. Besides gasoline refineries and booster stations there were Carbon Black plants. These plants refined carbon out of the oil. This black carbon dust that escaped (and a lot of it did escape) floated through the air and covered everything in the country side. The grass was not green, but black. The whiteface cattle were black, and we breathed in this carbon. One time I got sick and threw up black flakes of carbon along with the other "stuff."   In the spring we left Texas and moved with Dresser 5 times, to Pauls Valley, Duncan, back to Bowlegs, Guyman and to Garden City, Kansas. But, everywhere we moved we liked the place a little better. God was really with us!!

In Pauls Valley we lived in an "apartment" inside a flower nursery.   While living in Duncan, Dixie came to pick me up from work one day and backed the car over a gas meter and knocked it loose. It scared her to "death" but she turned the ignition off real soon and got out of the car.   The escaping gas made so much noise that some men not too far away heard it and came over and got the car off the meter and stopped the leak. It's a miracle that it didn't burst into flame and cause serious damage!   God was still looking out after us! Dixie's folks were living in Comanche at that time and so we visited often.

In Garden City we found a church and people we really cared about and grew closer to the Lord.   But from Garden City the US Marines gave us a call and I was drafted (that's right, I was drafted into the Marines.)   When I faced the draft board they asked me if I wanted to go into the Army, Navy, Air Force or Marines. I wouldn't answer them because I didn't want to go in any of them, and I thought that if I was going to be drafted God could put me where He wanted me ...so they said, "You are in the Marines!"   I really had a feeling that is where they would put me, and so they did.

On March 21, 1952 I became Pvt. Swain and set sail, from OKC on a train, to San Diego, Calif. When I arrived I was in for a "SHOCK." They took everything away from us that we had taken and we "donated" it to some " charity" ? They told us that while we were in Boot Camp we were not

26

even a citizen of the United States of America, "<u>and they</u> <u>treated us like that and we believed it!!!</u>" I had quite some experiences in boot, but I shot expert on the rifle range and became a squad leader, and briefly saw 2 other former Bowlegs classmates in other platoons at Boot Camp. Since I had been a carpenter before being drafted they didn't let me have a furlough like the others when Boot Camp was over but they said I was assigned to the Sea Bees, (CB's as some call it. It's official name is Construction Battalion and they construct all of the necessary buildings overseas in times of war) and I was held over several days until they had recruited enough persons to open a new class. After a week or so I was able to go home on a 10-day furlough. I guess all of the others probably were sent to Korea because I only saw one of the others after that and he had just returned from Korea.

I had been assigned to attend the "CB" school 40 miles west of Los Angeles at Port Hueneme, Calif. near Oxnard. Dixie had been about as "shook up" as I was about being separated and facing the unknowns and perils of war so she was determined to go to California with me. Not only was Dixie determined to go, but since I was Mother's only child, and she was a widow, she was determined to go also. What could I do? My monthly check was only $87 and my car payments were $95. I said no way! How could we pay rent, and live? They both said they would get a job. So I finally agreed to try. We sold everything we had accumulated and paid off the car and headed out to California. We traveled the old Highway 66 through Arizona and it followed the old gold mining trail through the mountains in the western part of the state. This road had been made for the Model T and Model A Fords, and believe me, it was narrow and dangerous. One "hair pen" curve was so sharp that some of the large buses had to back

27

up and make a sharper turn to get around it, and on one side, in many places, there was no shoulder and it was hundreds or thousands of feet to the bottom of the embankment. On our first return trip from California that section of I40 highway had just been opened. What a relief!

The first night in Port Hueneme we "slept" (stayed) in the car parked in a pecan orchard. The next day we went hunting for a cheap apartment, but in this wartime Navy town there was almost nothing available. We did find one garage apartment but it was $60 per month, and we couldn't afford that so we looked further. We did find an apartment ("really a chicken house") on the ocean beach, for $30, but-----it was filthy, filthy, filthy!!!! This Navy town during the war was flooded with sailors and Marines and there just wasn't anything available for us in our price range! So we hurried back to the garage apartment with hopes we could make it somehow. But, but, but a sailor was just walking out when we arrived, he had just rented it. Soooooo, we hurried back to the "chicken house!

The building was probably 50 to 60 feet long by 16 or 18 feet and divided into 5 apartments by a one, single thickness of Celetex partition (Celetex is a soft sheet of something 3/8 to 1/2 inch and probably not as strong as a piece of cardboard.) Our "apartment" was about 10 or 12 feet wide and 16 to 18 feet long and was divided into 2 rooms. You can imagine how little room we had in either room. And our "bed" was pushed against this wall on one side and the neighbor's was against it on the other side. Can you imagine?? Did I say bed??? It was not really a bed but a single layer of metal mesh hooked onto a frame only at the head and the foot just like a hammock. The very thin "mattress" (bed) bagged down in the middle and you couldn't stretch out straight, both Dixie and I were always rolled down into the middle in a ball. The place was so filthy that Dixie wouldn't move in without washing everything in the apartment, walls, ceiling, furniture, cabinets etc. We even took the stove apart and washed the burners! And, our neighbor had a dog on a rope just long enough for the dog to reach our back step. Can you imagine what our step looked like most of the time???

 As you can imagine all of this was very, very bad, except a couple of things. This apartment was directly on the beach and Dixie loved the beach. The first day there it was cloudy all day but Dixie spent most of it on the beach----- but the thing she didn't know was that despite being overcast, the harmful rays of the sun could come through and do their damage. By nightfall she was sunburned something awful and as red as the stripes in the flag. What a price she paid. The other good thing was that the owner's daughter had a little boy and she needed a baby sitter and Dixie got her job babysitting. The Bakersfield Tehachapi earthquake happened while we were in bed one night, about a hundred miles away, and it rocked us pretty good but we didn't even get up out of bed.

One problem "solved" and we had another. Mother now needed a job so we got a Los Angeles paper and searched the want adds. There were a couple of adds she was particular interested in. After checking the first one she wanted to see another one so we went to Beverly Hills where she thought the ad was for a cook, housemaid and/or a nanny for a Dr. Bedford. Mother had done this kind of work for years in OKC. But she had mistakenly misread the ad and it was an address on Bedford Dr. So we went to Bedford Drive, a very, very "ritzy" place in the heart of Beverly Hills. Mother went in while Dixie and I sat in the car. After a while mother came out and told us that the woman wanted us to come in and meet her. Mother said the woman had done something she was not suppose to do and that was she had been hired "on the spot" without consulting her husband, but the woman had felt sure that mother was the right one for the job. Well, Dixie and I went and immediately I saw an autographed photo of Winston Churchill and of Pres. F.D. Roosevelt sitting on the baby grand piano so I asked, "Do you know FDR?" She said, "He's my father-in-law."

Can you imagine how I felt, unexpectedly being in the home of James Roosevelt, the son of the president of the United States? The Roosevelts had three children, two boys and a girl and everything worked out real well for both parties. Dixie and I went to Beverly Hills almost every week end and, not that they are any better than us Okies, but if you lived back in the early 1950's can you imagine how many movie stars and famous people lived near by? Adolph Monju lived directly across the street, Liz Taylor, Dick Haymes and Woody Herman down the street, Betty Grable and Bing Crosby, not very far and many others I've forgotten; and who else I don't really know but I did see Will Rogers Jr., Randolph Scott, Georgie Jessell and Gov. Knight of California.

I did really well in the CB's Construction School which lasted some three months. Out of a class of 123 I came out in first place and got to choose my duty station here in the US. I had five places from which to choose and I immediately chose Seattle, WA, because that was pretty close to several of my family who lived in Portland, OR. Well, almost immediately I began to feel that I had made the wrong choice and I kept feeling worse and worse for about 30 minutes. Without ever thinking that there was a possibility I might be able to make a change I just happened to see the Sgt. and told him that I thought I had made the wrong choice. He told me the person second in line had not made his choice yet and that I could make a change. I immediately changed to San Francisco and just as soon as I made my choice the person second in line said he would take Seattle. WOW! God had been so good to me again! It so happened that at San Francisco they had no barracks and all of the soldiers lived off base and got expense allotment and even for their dependents. That would mean a lot and perhaps Dixie could go with me there too!

After my furlough was over Dixie and I started out to San Francisco. Of course, we didn't have enough money to make the trip to California and rent an apartment in San Fran and live for 2 weeks until my next check but we started out anyway. In Albuquerque someone ran into the back of our car and did some minor damage and he paid us off right on the spot. By this time The Roosevelts had moved to Pasadena and we went by to see Mother on the way to San Francisco. As we left she gave us $25 dollars. (We drove all day through the desert and when we got to San Francisco and stepped out of the car it seemed like we were at the North Pole!) When we got our first check in San Francisco we actually had less than one dollar. God was really looking out for us!!

The apartment we lived in was about as bad but different from the one we lived in California. The only window we had was on the back alley. There were several apartments in the building and I think only men lived in the apartments. I never saw any women. There was a long hall and there was not a (real) bathroom. There was a stool and sink in one room and down the hall in another room there was a bathtub. And guess who got the job of keeping them clean??? We found out that one of the men who lived in there was from Scotland, Ark and had grown up with mother...small world!!! Well after 6 or 8 months we found another apartment, which used to be a garage. In San Fran most of the houses were upstairs, built over the garages because of the limited space. The back windows of this garage apartment open onto a beautiful little back yard not much bigger than the apartment but there was green grass, sunlight, flowers and the first morning when we awoke we could hear birds singing. Dixie said that was the most beautiful sound she had ever heard!

We saw and did lots of things in San Francisco. We went to Golden Gate Park often. It was very nice and spacious. Dixie worked in the edge of China Town not far from Fisherman's Wharf. . We went to the ocean often but it was too cold to swim in. One night the fog was so thick that you couldn't even see the roadway. I had to open my door and look down to see the road. The fog was under the car so thick it looked like a river. We were only driving about 5 miles an hour and soon I saw a car coming down my side of the boulevard, but I didn't see him until he was probably about 20 feet away. Good thing we were going so slow, he quickly turned his car and jumped the divider to the other side! ... We attended church about a block from where Patty Hurst was later arrested at Mission and Morris Street. Sometimes we'd go down on skid row and look around. One day a man got his throat cut real bad (not while we were there) but some person on skid row took a tooth pick and wove the vein back together enough to keep him from bleeding to death until the ambulance arrived. The newspaper reporter checked up on this person and found out he had been a famous doctor in Boston but was now down on skid row. This man's life is a perfect example of why I never drank or gambled. You never know what just one little drink or gamble may lead to. The big forest fires are usually started by just one little match or spark. But soon they rage out of control and destroy everything in their path. And so it is with many a life, they soon are consumed and destroyed and it all started by just one "little" act which they never imagine could happen to them!

We went to Oakland every Saturday night to the Youth For Christ and "accidently" ran onto our friend, Don Willingham. Back then there were service men everywhere and Youth for Christ gave one free telephone call to a lucky service man. This sailor walked upon the stage and Dixie recognized him. I tried to signal for him to come over where we were but he ignored us. Finally after I kept on signaling he came over and was he SURPRISED!!! It was the only time he had ever been there! One time we were crossing the Bay Bridge and Helen Willingham's sister was with us. She was really, really homesick. I was following a car with a Missouri tag and I said there's a car from Missouri. She said I'd just "die" if it was someone I knew. I pulled up alongside and it happened to be one of her best friends. She almost did die!!! After we crossed the bridge we both stopped and visited for a while.

My Studebaker car sometimes vapor locked. That meant the gasoline had turned to vapor before it went through the fuel pump, usually because it was too hot, and the pump wouldn't pump gas into the carburetor. Well one day it stopped right in the middle of the bay bridge. You can imagine what that did to the traffic. I used to take wet rags and put on the fuel line and try to cool it down enough to turn the vapors back to gasoline but I had learned that I could just unscrew the gas line and the vapors would escape and then tighten the line back up and it would run. So I Just jumped out of the car, got my wrench and loosened the line, tightened it back up, jumped in the car and we were on our way. Also on our first trip to San Fran that Studebaker had vapor locked right out in the middle of the desert in New Mexico and it took a long, long time to get it unlocked just using wet rags.

A little later Dixie's dad had an operation and she came back to Okla. While she was gone I had to go to the rifle range about 30 miles away. As I've said at that time we were driving a Studebaker and there weren't many of them around and hardly any garages. Well, I was almost to the range and my automatic transmission went out...and would you know... there (just happened) to be a Studebaker Garage right where my transmission went out. God has looked out for us all of our lives. We also met Bob and Janie Richter in San Fran.   They and Don and Helen Willingham were, and have been probably, our two closest friendly couples. Us and the Willinghams have spent many times together at Tenkiller Lake in the summers, we visited them and they visited us and we spent our 25 wedding anniversary with them at Corpus Christy, Texas. And Bob and Janie have visited us here in OKC and we have visited them in California. Incidentally Don and Helen who had been missionaries in many parts of the world were killed (stabbed to death) about 2 years ago. An arrest has just been made this Feb. 2013 for the murder.

After 2 years in the Marines I was discharged and we came back to Bowlegs in 1954. I decided to build Mamma and Mother a new house in Bowlegs. It was a small 2-bedroom house with bath and a garage. I did everything about the building except the electric wiring. I even built the window units and put in the sewer. It took me 9 weeks. About the time I finished a former classmate came by and offered me a job for an oil company at Francis, Ok. We bought a small trailer house (with NO BATH) and moved there. That didn't work out too well and several months later Garland Shaffer's father-in-law wanted me to turn a building (a house where he kept his honey and sold it) into an apartment. So we pulled the trailer to Putnam City and I worked on the apartment in Bethany. After I finished that job I worked on some houses near the Zoo. Soon I got a call from Tinker to go to work on a sheet metal apprentice training program.

We moved our trailer to Midwest City, just about where the old Furrs Cafeteria used to be. We soon traded our trailer for the equity in a house at 307 N. Key. I went to work at Tinker and made $1.37 per hour. That would hardly pay our bills. At that time my friend Garland Shaffer had some penny gumball machines that he needed to get rid of and I took them. Every month I got about $40 dollars of pennies out of the machines and that was our grocery money, $10 per week. (Incidentally, did you know that we use to have money worth only one tenth of a penny? They were called mills...it took ten of them to make a penny) In about a month, after I went to work at Tinker, Terri was born.

When I went to work at Tinker the head doctor was Dr. Capps. He had been the doctor at Bowlegs when I was growing up. Also my old coach was in charge of the civilian activities there and he later became mayor of Midwest City. Also Mr. Emerson who had started the School at Bowlegs and was there for 25 years was now at Kerr Jr. High and spent 25 years there. And Charles Meyers who had been at Bowlegs was now band director at Del City and Mr. and Mrs. Moore were teachers as well as my old girl friend Margaret Mitchell Williams. A little later Bill Swain coached at Del City and Coach Manning's wife was from Bowlegs. It seemed there were Bowlegs people everywhere, some others lived as close as 1/2 mile.

Two years later Ginger was born...and in June of 1957 we moved to 2237 S. Webster. We were so far out then that 15th Street wasn't even paved. There was no Carl Albert School. The road we drove down to our acreage was really not a road. A bulldozer had pushed its way through the trees and there were still stumps in parts of the "Road"!!! There was no bridge or culvert across the creek and when it rained we had to leave our car and walk to the house. The trees, vegetation, under growth and downed trees were so thick that it took me three different tries to get across the north end of our five acres. I finally got down on my knees and crawled part way along the creek that ran across the property. The land out here was selling for $300 an acre at that time and now...it's selling for $40,000 an acre. It took about 40 years before I got all of the clearing done on this property that I wanted. We had moved the house that I helped Claud build in Bowlegs in about 1943 or 1944 to 2237 S. Webster. We were going to live in it a few years and then build a new one. In 1960 Billy was born. Our family was now complete. After numerous remodelings (probably a dozen or more) we are still living in that house. In the meantime, I had built Mother and Mamma another new house on this property. In 1963 Bill and I were working on Mamma's house. Bill was only three years old but he could drive a 16 penny nail all of the way in and never bend it. I'll bet some of those boards have perhaps 25 or 30 nails in them that he drove in. That was the day that Pres. Kennedy was killed.

This scroll of the King James version of the HOLY BIBLE , including both Old and New testements, is believed to be the
only copy of the entire BIBLE ever written in its entirety on
one, continuous unspliced scroll. It was handscribed by
William O. Swain. The time required for writing covered a 33
months period from August 1977 to May 1980.

The overall measurement of this manuscript is 3,485 feet, unrolled it would stretch some 2/3 mile in length. It contains
109,824 lines of writing consisting of over 3/4 million words
and 3.5+ million letters. Placed end to end these lines would
reach 947,232 inches which equals about 14.95 miles in length.
This BIBLE weighs 50 pounds. It requires approximately 4 hours
to roll the scroll from beginning to end.

William O. "Bill" Swain

In 1977 I started writing the Scroll of the Bible and completed it 3 years later. (see Exhibit 1, page 257) In 1989, 1999 and1990 I worked at Falls Creek Baptist Assembly near Turner Falls. I passed out some 40,000 poems to the young people who attended there. I first attended Falls Creek in 1941. It is the world's largest Christian youth assembly. Mr. William Ryan Swain was born while I was working there. In Jr. High I started carving some. We had been down to Atwood visiting my father's sister, Molly Henry, and her husband showed me a carving he had made of George Washington...and I thought, "I think I could do better than that"...so I started. I carved the largest horse standing on its hind legs while I was in high school. When I started going with Dixie she wanted to take it to Holdenville where she was attending beauty college and I told her she couldn't handle it without breaking it...but she insisted...oh I won't break it she said. I let her take it.   She brought it back to me in 4 or 5 pieces.... I carved some little boots and saddles while in high school (sort of a little ornament) that you pinned on your lapel. I think I carved 13 of them but the kids would steal them off of my coat and I think I wound up with only 2 left...I think Ginger might have one of them but I don't know where the other one went to...One day, Ginger brought home a little chair made out of a coke can. I started making chairs out of the coke cans and then I made some out of smaller cans...and then I made some even smaller out of really small cans. I also carved quite a few boots and a few other items.

Although I said that I didn't know of any girl getting pregnant when I was in school it wasn't long after until I began to hear of some getting pregnant, and one was the piano player in church. That really hurt me. A little later I decided to write a story and make a movie, which I hoped would send a message to any who saw it and heeded it. In

1959 and 1960 I did make a crude movie called "THE CLIFF". It was not a professional production but I hoped to use it as sort of a script to get a professional production made...but I never accomplished that. I did show the movie around locally probably 35 or 40 times. I did make another movie called "MY CHURCH".

I also wrote a book about my life at Bowlegs called "BOWLEGS EIGHTY YEARS AFTER". I also wrote a book titled "SOMEWHERE OVER THERE". The setting was in France during WWII, sort of a war/love story. I have always been interested in poetry and I have written well over 100 poems. The subject range varies. I have written a poem about all of my family members except the great grand kids (Guess I'll have to get busy on them), many about Christianity, and for young folks, a few funny ones and I have written poems about Bowlegs and my experiences there and have written and given poems at most of the annual Bowlegs banquets and our class parties since 1986, and I have written a few songs.

As I've said several times before God has been very good to me, and I wouldn't change anything (well maybe a thing or two) if I could. I wouldn't change my forefathers, my parents, my wife, my children, my in-laws, where I grew up, the jobs I've had, where I've lived ...and where I now live or anything about my life. As I've said before I never regret that I didn't graduate from college. I've never made a big salary, the most I have ever made in one year was $25,000, and I've really never desired to have more. Of course I'd take it if it came along. I have never gone hungry a day in my life and never been in want for anything I really needed. When I look around at people, and neighbors and acquaintances and see the messes that some of their lives and families and kids are in, I feel so blessed and wonder how and why God has been so good to me!!! You know, the Lord has only promised us four score and 10 years (70 years) and in 3 months I'll already have a bonus of 15 extra years...and who knows how many more I'll have. Maybe someday I'll know why.

I heard, and felt, the bombing of the Murray Building in which some 160 or 170 people were killed. We just escaped the big tornado that came through and killed so many. The weather report said the tornado was headed for 15th and Post Rd but it turned when it reached the western part of Midwest City and missed us. Thank the Lord!!! I did stand on the porch and listen to the tornado that went through 44th and Post a few years ago as it missed us about a mile. And 3 years ago when about 40 houses were burned down the fire started about 1/4 mile from our house and came as close as our neighbor's yard fence.

In 2008 I was back in Scotland, Ark on November 5, mother's birthday, and visited my father's grave. That was 80 years to the day that he was buried...on mother's 18th birthday. Last year Ginger took me back to Scotland and we did some research on family members trying to find old graveyards and graves. Also we visited the site where I was born, where mother was born, where my dad died, the old house had been built by my granddad W.R. O'Neal but 3 years ago a tornado had totally, completely blown it away and also several house near by where several of Mamma's family had lived, Mintie Hall, her sister...Jeff Casinger...Thomas Casinger and others...but Granddad's brother Poley O'Neal's house was not damaged. In 2008, I also went in the house where I was born, and to my surprise, no one had lived in it since 1987 but everything was still in the house. Since the last Kincannon family member who lived in the house had died no one else had

39

lived in there but everything was still in place. The dishrag was still hanging on the wall, dishes, cooking utensils, plates and silverware were still there. The record book that everyone signs at the funeral was still laying on the table. The beds and quilts still there, chest drawers full, furniture, everything still there and had been there since 1987. It seemed so strange that everything had just been left. But we went up on the hill to my Aunt Minnie's house (she lived to be 100) and her house had not been occupied for probably 25 or 30 years and it was still there...but it was empty except a few boxes of items left. I guess there are not enough people, especially young people, who are left around Scotland who are interested in staying or living there.

We then went down to the diamond mine in Murfreesboro to find a fortune of diamonds. We didn't find any diamonds...but we did find some pearls... some "pearls of great price"...great MEMORIES!!!

Bill Swain

PS...Well, we are still in the old house (after a dozen or more remodelings) and that doesn't make my Dear Dixie too happy!!!   Now you know "REST OF THE STORY"

PPS...I believe that I have been privileged to live in the greatest part of American (U.S.) history. That would be during the 20th Century. Many of our early forefathers suffered greatly. They moved slowly westward many times going into areas where white men had never been before, into the wilds where everything they ate and everything that it took to sustain life had to be taken from the land. Some of the things they ate to survive would "curl your hair"! There were no stores, no roads, no houses, no money and nothing to buy if you had any money, but in these early days there was not even any money to be had. The U.S. dollar had not even come into existence yet. They lived entirely off of the land if they survived. There was no retirement, no welfare, no Social Security...you were on your own.

By the time I came along most of these things had changed, and in most cases, living was much easier. A basic knowledge and reverence for God was implanted in our government. Our coins so stated IN GOD WE TRUST. The date on each coin or dollar bill (2013 or whatever date that is on it) is a witness that some 2013 years ago God sent Jesus Christ into the world because He loved us so. We date all of our history from this event. Everything has a date, your birth certificate, your marriage license, your abstract and everything has a date it was born or was made. All legal things require a date...And what does the date of your new 2013 automobile really mean??

I never went hungry a day in my life. We didn't even lock our doors at night. I hitchhiked all around the country with anyone who would pick me up. For a while Ford cars didn't even use a key in order for the engine to run. It had a switch just like a light switch. You just flipped the switch and pushed the starter to crank the engine. But it's a different world today. I think just before the turn of the century, probably in the 70's and 80's it seemed that things (morals, marriage standards, family life, our society, our leaders, our government) started on a down swing and today I am concerned for our future, our children, grandchildren and our nation. My only hope and comfort lies in the fact that I believe that God is in control of everything.

THE REASON
by Bill Swain

"Why do you write poetry?"
Someone asked me, just today;
The reason is that I believe
I really have something to say!

A poem is really a message, or song,
Without the musical score...
Some love the rhyme and message it brings;
To others...it's just a "bore."

We can write long speeches and stories
And do our best to converse,
But oft times as much, or more can be said
In a very short poem or verse.

I hope I have not offended you,
Or wasted your valuable time,
By sharing my innermost thoughts with you,
Spelled out in verse and rhyme!

FAITH

JESUS AND THE HOLY SCRIPTURES

The following is a list of information, teachings, and preachings that I have assembled from various authors now unknown to me.
Bill Swain

John 1:1, Jesus came unto His own and His own received Him not. They rejected Him as the Messiah.
In John 5:29, He told them to search the scriptures because they are they which testify of Me. If they had searched the scriptures with an open heart they would have found they were all about Jesus:

In Genesis	He was the seed of woman
Exodus	The Passover Lamb
Leviticus	High Priest
Numbers	A Cloud by day, pillar of fire by night
Deuteronomy	A Prophet
Joshua	Captain of their salvation
In Judges	Law giver and Great Judge
Ruth	Kinsman Redeemer
Samuel	Trusted Prophet
In Kings & Chron	Reigning King
Ezra	Faithful Scribe
Nehemiah	Re-builder of broken down walls of their life
Ester	Their Mordecai
In Job	The Day Spring
Psalms	Their Lord and Shepherd
Prov & Eccle	Wisdom
Isaiah	Prince of Peace
Jeremiah	Righteous Branch
Lamentations	Weeping Prophet
Ezekiel	Wheel a'turning
Daniel	4th Man in the fire
Hosea	The Bridegroom that marries the backslider
Joel,	Baptizer with Holy Spirit and fire
In Amos	Our Burden Bearer
Obadiah	Mighty Savior
Jonah	A Foreign Missionary
Micah	Messenger with the beautiful feet carrying the Gospel
Nahum	Avenger of God's Elect
Habakkuk	Evangelist crying for revival
Zephaniah	Restorer of God's lost heritage
Haggai	Cleansing Fountain
Zachariah	Righteous Father
Malachi	Son of Righteousness with healing in His wings

Genesis 3:15 tells us that Jesus had to be the seed of a woman. Galatians 4:4 tells us that happened.

Genesis 12:3 says He was to be the seed of Abraham. Matthew 1:1 tells us that is true.

Genesis 17:19 tells us He had to be the seed of Isaac. Luke 3:34 says that happened.

Genesis 49:10 says He was to be from the tribe of Judah. Luke 3:33 verifies that.

Micah 5:2 says He will be born in Bethlehem. Luke 2:4 records Jesus' birth there.

Isaiah 7:14 tells us He will be born of a virgin. Luke 1:31 says He was.

Hosea 11:1 says He will go down to Egypt. Matthew 2:15 tells of this happening.

Psalms 78:2 tells of His speaking in parables. Matthew 13:34 tells this fact.

Isaiah 61:1 says He will come to heal the broken hearted. Luke 4:18 tells of this ministry.

Isaiah 53:3 tells us He will be rejected by His own. John 1:11 records this is true.

Isaiah 53:7 says He will be silent before His accusers. Mark 15:5 says Jesus answered not a word.

Psalms 22:1 tells us He will be forsaken by God. Matthew 27:46 records Jesus own words.

Isaiah 53:9 says He will be buried with the rich. Matthew 27:60 says this is true.

Psalms 49:15 tells us Jesus will be redeemed.   Mark 16:9 tells of Jesus' resurrection.

Once you see Him, not with your eyes but with your heart, you are changed.

Isaiah, When he saw His glory he shouted, "Woe is me. I am a man of unclean lips!"

Peter said, "I am a sinful man."

John fell at His feet.

Paul saw more in blindness than he saw before he was blinded. He was transformed from Saul to Paul.

In the New Testament writings:

Matthew saw Him as the Messiah,

Mark, as the Wonder Worker,

Luke, as the Son of Man,

John, as the Son of God,

Acts presents Him as the ascended Lord who sent the Holy Spirit,

Romans, the Great Justifier,

Corinthians, as the giver of the gifts of the Holy Spirit,
Galatians, as the Man who set us free,
Ephesians, as the Christ of great riches,
Philippians, as the God who meets our every need,
Colossians, as the fullness of the Godhead,
Thessalonians, as the Coming King,
Timothy, as the mediator between God and Man,
Titus, as the Faithful Pastor,
Philemon, as the Friend that sticks closer than a brother,
Hebrews, as the Blood that washed away our sin,
James, as the Great Physician,
Peter, as the Chief Shepherd,
Peter, as Everlasting Love,
Jude, as the Lord coming down with 10,000's of His saints,
Revelation, as the King of Kings and the Lord of Lords.

Revelation is the unveiling of Jesus Christ. Revelation is the capstone of all previous Revelation. Many of the truths begun in Genesis are concluded in Revelation.
In Genesis was the beginning of heaven and earth. In Revelation is the consummation of heaven and earth.
In Genesis was the dawn of Satan and his activities. In Revelation the doom of Satan.
In Genesis the entrance of sin and the curse. In Revelation the exit of sin and the curse.
In Genesis the tree of life is relinquished. In Revelation it is regained.
In Genesis death enters. In Revelation death exits.
In Genesis sorrow begins. In Revelation it is banished forever.

We must not stop with just the Gospels because we would not have all of the truth. In Revelation the majesty of Jesus Christ is revealed. In the gospels we have;
His humiliation, In Revelation His glorification,
In the gospels His death, in Revelation He rebukes death,
In the gospels his enemies applaud, in Revelation they appeal,
In the gospels He is Savior, in Revelation He Sentences the evil ones,
In the gospels He was pierced, in Revelation He is praised,
In the gospels He was a victim, in Revelation the Victor,
In the gospels He received a cross, in Revelation He received a crown,
In the gospels He received the thorns, in Revelation He received the Throne,
In the gospels He was a criminal, in Revelation He was the Conqueror,

In the gospels He accepted the guilt, in Revelation He accepted the glory.

In Revelation God gives His compliments, His complaints and His commands to the churches:

Here are His complaints:

Some had purity but no passion,

They labored but not in love,

They had a duty but no devotion,

They had a message but no meaning,

They spoke from their head but not from the heart,

They did service but without any Spirit,

They had a practice but no power,

They practiced separation without inspiration,

They preached justification but had no joy,

They preached regeneration but had no rejuvenation,

They preached soul winning but had no soul stirring,

They were popular but powerless.

Jesus said I am against you, you have left your first love. The furnace is there but the fire is out.

Doing the Kings business will never make up for neglecting the King.

After Jesus was resurrected He ascended back to heaven to pick up everything He had laid aside. The Father said this is my beloved son in whom I am well pleased. He put the robe of righteousness back on Him and he sat down at the right hand of the Father. He made the journey back from misery to majesty, from guilt to glory. Jesus was given a name which is above every name. One day every tongue will confess that Jesus Christ is the Lord. Here are some names He is called:

1st John 2:1, the Advocate,

Rev 1:8, The Almighty,

Rev 3:14, The A-Men,

Rev 21:6, The Alpha and the Omega,

Daniel 7:9, The Ancient of Days,

Col 3:11, The All and All,

Heb 12:2, The Author and Finisher of our faith,

Matt 3:7, The Beloved Son,

John 6:35, The Bread of Life,

Jeremiah 8:22, The Balm of Gilead,

1st Peter 2:25, Bishop of our souls,

Rev 22:16, The Bright and Morning Star,

John 3:29, The Bridegroom,

1 Peter 5:4, Chief Shepherd,
Heb 2:10, Captain of our Salvation,
Isaiah 9:6, Counselor, Prince of Peace,
Isaiah 28:16, Cornerstone,
Luke 1:78, Day spring from on high,
John 10:7, The Door,
Romans 11:26, The Deliverer,
2 Pet 1:19, Daystar,
Matt 1:23, Emmanuel,
1 John 5;11, Everlasting Life,
Isaiah 9:6 Everlasting Father,
Psalms 90:2, From Everlasting to Everlasting,
Hew 6:20, The Forerunner,
Heb 4:14, Great High Priest,
John 1:29, The Lamb of God,
John 9:5, The Light of the World,
1 Tim 2:5 Mediator between God and man,
Solomon 2:1, The Rose of Sharon, the Lily of the Valley,
Psalms 24:7, King of Glory,
Psalms 23:1, Our Shepherd.

Yes, Jesus has a name which is above every name! Philippians 2: 5-11 tells us that Jesus humbled Himself and became obedient unto death. Because of this God has given Him a name which is above every name and someday every tongue will confess that Jesus Christ is Lord. Even at the early age of 12 years when Jesus entered the temple, Luke 2:46, 47, tells us this young boy was sitting in the midst of the doctors talking with them. Never had they seen one so young and so sweet with such knowledge. Can't you just imagine some of the questions they asked Him.
Like, son what is your name?
Well, on my mother's side my name is Jesus... but on my Father's side they call me Emmanuel.
How old are you?
On my mother's side I'm 12 years old, but on my Father's side...I've just always been.
Where are you from?
On my mother's side I'm from Bethlehem...but on my Father's side it's New Jerusalem.
What are your plans?
On my mother's side I'll be crucified...but on my Father's side in 3 days

I'll arise and sit at my Father's side.

All that heard Him were astonished at His answers.

He was the Son of God, yet the Son of man. And I can't help but wonder how Joseph must have felt, when through an open door one day he heard his Son reply,

He said, "You see, I am the King of Kings, that's on my Father's side."

The grave could not hold Him. He is The KING of KINGS!

A HUNDRED TO ONE

I heard this news on TV just the other day,
I think they were talking about nine-eleven;
But I don't agree with the report I heard...
Everyone thinks they are going to heaven.

Only one in a hundred in the survey taken
Believe when they die they will go to hell;
But the daily news of murder, rape and hate
Has a very dismal and sad story to tell.

Why do most people think they will go to heaven?
Because...because...because they don't really know;
They think perhaps if they do enough good works...
They'll make it...but they really just hope it's so.

How can we know and be sure of heaven
In this sinful and wicked world we are living in?
The Bible says many are called but few get to go
Because we are naturally creatures of sin.

In Matthew 7-21 Jesus says not everyone will enter
Who calls me Lord, and does wonderful works;
That applies to all doctors, lawyers, politicians, cooks,
Engineers, all common people, preachers and clerks.

It's not by our own good works of righteousness,
No it's not...Jesus says we must be born again;
It's by His grace, through faith in His sacrifice
That we're saved from hell and the wrath of sin.

Jesus said, "I am the Way the Truth and the Life,
No one can come to the Father but by Me."
Salvation cannot be earned, it's a gift from God,
Paid for by Jesus death on the cross at Calvary.

ADAM AND EVE

Many years ago as I recall,
In a beautiful dwelling place,
A lovely couple lived all alone;
Their memory I can never erase.

There were many things for them to see
And many things for them to do;
They could eat most anything they wished,
And were forbidden of only two.

Now these two are really just one, some say;
Well, take it either way You choose
Because either way, they're going to pay,
Either way they're going to loose!

Not so, she thought, when Eve took a look
And reasoned it out in her mind;
The fruit, I see looks so good to me
I'll bet it's the tastiest you'll ever find.

And the tree is as beautiful as you'll ever see
And it is so pleasant to my eye;
It's really one to be desired by me,
Why Can't I?   Why Can't I?   Why?

You can.   Believe me.   Go on ahead,
Her "friend" began to advise,
Everything I see looks good to me,
And don't forget, it will make you wise.

51

How thrilling it was to make her own choice
And not have her freedom of reason perturbed,
After all, she could think, and feel, and see;
She would not let her thoughts be disturbed.

So she plucked with glee some fruit from the tree
And gave one or two to her man,
He took a big bite and swallowed it down
And threw the rest of it back in her hand.

Like a bolt of lightening, as quick as a wink,
Like an arrow shot threw the heart,
His eyes rolled around and bugged 'way out;
He was "wise" now...but not very smart.

"Hey woman," he yelled, "Look what you did...
And what happened to that other Dude?
I can see everything so clearly now,
Hey...we're running around in the nude!"

"Our worldly wisdom has let us down,
With regret, we apologize to all;
When our Maker speaks, obey what He says,
Our fleshly wisdom has led to our fall."

"So, no matter what others may argue or say,
If God said it, believe me, It's TRUE.
If it's something condemned or forbidden by HIM,
That's something you'd better not do!"

BE SMART! DON'T START

To The Searching Heart

There's a scourge in our land that's destroying our heart,
The use of drugs and alcohol.......Be Smart! Don't Start!.

It's tearing many families and happy homes apart,
The use of drugs and alcohol......Be Smart! Don't Start!

It's often glorified in music and movies called art,
The use of drugs and alcohol........Be Smart! Don't Start!

Addicts are now much younger as revealed by our chart,
Stoned on drugs and alcohol.........Be Smart! Don't Start!

Some start at the drug store and some the grocery mart,
This use of drugs and alcohol.........Be Smart! Don't Start!

Your life may seem sweet but soon will turn very tart,
By using drugs and alcohol.............Be Smart! Don't Start!

If you continue I guarantee it will upset your "apple cart"...
The use of drugs and alcohol..........Be Smart! Don't Start!

Your life will be wrecked when struck by the poison dart
Of drugs and alcohol......................Be Smart! Don't Start!

You may loose family and friends or perhaps a sweetheart
By using drugs and alcohol.............Be Smart! Don't Start!

You may forfeit becoming President.....or another Mozart
By using drugs and alcohol.............Be Smart! Don't Start!

You will be denied that which God wants to impart
By using drugs and alcohol.............Be Smart! Don't Start!

53

If you wish to follow wisdom you must immediately depart
The use of drugs and alcohol..........Be Smart! Don't Start!

Renounce, now and forever, and flee as fast as the hart
The use of drugs and alcohol..........Be Smart! Don't Start!

Vow to never be the problem but a stalwart rampart
Against drugs and alcohol..............Be Smart! Don't Start!

Be all that you can be by upholding your part
Against drugs and alcohol...............Be Smart! Don't Start!

CHOICES

Have you ever gone through the cafeteria food line
And found something delicious and great,
But your friend didn't like it at all and said to you,
"That's one of the worst things I ever ate."

How could you and your friends have tastes so different;
Aren't you glad you can choose according to your taste?
If someone had to pick out each and everything I ate
I think perhaps a lot of things would go to waste.

Let's look at life, like going through the cafeteria line,
Where there are dozens of choices to make,
Usually we choose what we think will be best,
Never- the -less, sometimes we make a big mistake.

Wouldn't it be great if we could accept with grace
Others whose differences we don't understand;
It takes all the different parts to make a human body,
Every eye, ear, nose, leg and hand.

And so it is in the course of human life,
Everyone has their own likes, gifts and personality;
We may be good friends but see or do things different,
And there's positively no reason to feel guilty.

Everyone is different though made by God's own hands,
In His family there's no one else like you, but you;
But we can all unite and be one in His service
And do the job God created us to do.

If we could only understand and accept other's differences,
Like everyone's choices in the cafeteria line,
I think our world would be better and happier for us,
If we follow the same rule we do when we set down to dine.

DEAR LORD
A Song

I want to thank you, Lord, for all that you have done,
I want to praise your Name for You're God's only Son,
I want to trust You more for You're the only one
That satisfies the heart and sets the Spirit free.

I want to see You, Lord, and look on Your dear face,
I want to touch You, Lord, and feel Your sweet embrace,
I want to thank You, Lord, for mercy and for grace
That satisfies the heart and sets the Spirit free.

I want to live, Dear Lord, where all the Saints rejoice,
I want to ask You, Lord, why I became Your choice,
I want to hear, Dear Lord, the sweetness of the voice
That satisfies the heart and sets the Spirit free.

DECISIONS

Many things happen in this old world
That will affect us the rest of our life,
Like education, occupation, and where we live,
And the mate we have chosen for life.

The choices we make may affect others as well,
But oft' times we fail to see why,
And we may never realize where a decision may lead
No matter how hard we try.

Let's think for a moment of a few decisions
That have shaped the world we live in;
What if Columbus had failed to sail the high seas...
And what about Adam and Eve's sin?

What about our war of Independence, and WW II,
And the jets that fly in the sky;
Our lives have been shaped by decisions, decisions,
And we don't always understand why.

It is true; decisions are the determining factor
Of the road we will travel in life,
Some for the good...some do turn out bad,
That lead to heartache, failure and strife.

What about decisions that affect the "hereafter"
When time shall be no more?
Have you made that decision, have you chosen the one
Who will lead you to that "golden shore?"

JESUS CHRIST is the "ONE"...the only "ONE."
He's calling! He's calling! Don't delay!
If you haven't made that decision, and accepted HIM,
Will you trust JESUS today?

DEMOCRACY

You know we like to praise our form of democracy
As being the answer to our way of life;
We say we have this form of government
To make laws that settle our problems and strife.

Wouldn't you think that people who promote freedom
Would do what is best for all of mankind,
But freedom is an important two-way street
And it seems our government is totally blind.

They now have made laws to promote homosexuality;
One of the worst sins in the Bible, we find,
And because they do not wish to obey God's word
He has given them over to a reprobate mind.

Democracy, alone, is certainly not the answer...
And to think so is very wrong and absurd,
When people who govern and make the laws of our land
Have no belief in, or respect for God's Holy Word.

And what is happening to our citizens and country?
We have more and more problems every day;
Our jails are more than full; they're overflowing.
And more and more lives and families are in disarray.

Over half of the people don't think marriage is sacred,
They just live together, like the prodigal son with the hogs,
Decent and honorable family life is quickly vanishing,
Much of our Christian heritage has gone to the dogs.

Home life is being destroyed by our choices,
If we survive, Christian families are a "must" in our city;
Many children don't even know who their father is...
God have mercy... on them and us... what a pity!

The whole world is in a constant state of turmoil,
There's wars and hatred and conflicts on every hand,
The daily news is about thievery, rapes and murders
In every city, of any size, here in our own land.

I believe God in our lives is the only answer,
Oh, how He wants in but there is no room,
Many want God out of their lives and everything else,
If we do take Him out... it will be our doom.

Democracy is no more moral than its people,
And certainly not the laws made by disbelieving men,
But they can be if we follow God's Word He has given,
And when our lives are obedient...only then...only then.

I believe Christ's return is the answer to this problem,
Someday soon, He'll come to take His bride away;
Like it was in the sinful and wicked days of Noah,
He'll return...are you ready...it could be today?

DESPAIR

It isn't just the words you said
But how you turned and...tossed you head,
And gave that look that cut my heart...
And drove us one more step apart.

You don't really, sometimes, say a thing
But it's the discontent you bring;
Everything I say...everything I do
Seems to, somehow, cut you through and through.

It's different now, not like before,
You hardly notice, anymore,
You never listen when I say,
"I have a special need, today!"

Oh, how I hurt...Oh can't you see
The pain and fear that troubles me;
My heart is breaking...aching so,
Oh, can't you see? Oh, don't you know?

I hardly even feel alive,
We must have help if we survive,
Our good intents seem all in vain
And every hour is filled with pain.

I feel neglected...all alone,
The joys of life are now all gone,
I have no trust, nor hope, today,
My pain just never goes away.

Oh, is there hope...please, Lord, hear me
And help these blinded eyes to see;
Draw us together like before;
Renew our Faith...our Love restore!

DO YOU BELIEVE?

It's easy to say I believe in Jesus,
But what do you believe about Him;
Do you believe He came from heaven to earth,
As we sing about in the hymn?

Do you believe He was a good and kind person,
Because that is what others have said,
And what do you mean when you say you believe;
That He actually raised people from the dead?

Do you believe He healed the lame and sick...
Do you believe that in your heart or just your head;
Do you believe Jesus was the Son of God,
And other Bible stories you have read.

Do you believe Jesus was crucified?
That He died on the cruel cross for you,
We can believe with our mind but not our heart...
And that meaning of "believe" is not true.

What does the Bible say, and what does it mean,
And what does His Word mean to me...
We must obey the real true meaning of "believe"
Before we can be saved and set free.

Matt. 2:19 says even the Devil believes these facts,
But he hasn't committed his heart to the Lord,
We must believe with our heart, trust only in Jesus,
Like He tells us to do in His Word.

EAT, DRINK AND BE MERRY

I know most of you have heard this old saying,
"Eat, drink and be merry, today,
For we know not what will happen tomorrow,
And don't worry what others have to say.

"For we only have just one lifetime to live,
To enjoy all of life's pleasures we can,
So let's do everything that fancies our mind,
That brings fulfillment to a mortal man."

I know this may sound good at the very first thought
But there's a whole other side of the story,
Since our life on this earth is just the beginning
I think it's time to discuss the Lord and His Glory.

The Bible says our heart is deceitful and desperately wicked
Because we are born under the curse of sin;
If we honestly search our heart and accept Jesus as Lord
A whole new life in Jesus Christ can begin.

Now, a foolish man is right in his own eyes,
And in his heart he says there is no God,
But he must accept Jesus in this present life
Because it's too late when you rest beneath the sod.

What does it profit, my friend, if a man
Gains all the world but looses his own soul;
To loose one's own soul for worldly gain and pleasure,
That's too much of a highly price toll!

He that believeth in Jesus is not condemned,
"He that believeth not is condemned already," says He;
But Jesus waits with loving, arms outstretched,
"Oh sinner come, come unto me and I'll set you free."

FALLS CREEK

Written in 1990

The Young People's Place.   This Baptist Youth Camp in Oklahoma is
the world's largest Christian Camp, serving over 30,000 young people per
summer. There is now a new 7,000-seat air conditioned auditorium.

Tell me, what is Falls Creek...what do you do...
Is it a week vacation for your friends and you?
   It's hot summer days and preaching and classes,
   Contests for T shirts,,,and fancy sunglasses.

It's meeting folks, playing jokes and exchanging names,
Swimming and hiking and endless ball games.
   It's icees and cold drinks and the grocery store,
   Ice cream and hot pizzas...and a whole lot more!

It's very special places that some folks seek,
Like the Devil's bathtub and parks by the creek;
   It's six-thousand youths for five weeks in a row
   Roaming up hills and down hills, wandering to and fro;

Milling masses, all classes, the grounds teeming with kids,
No short pants or dresses... the rule now forbids.
   There's a few other things young folks like to do...
   Hunting boy friends and girl friends, to name you just two.

Searching eyes...anxious faces...boy meets girl,
Long walks...small talk. heads in a whirl,
   A few stolen kisses, many freely imparted,
   Some romances ended before they are started.

A few heartaches, heartbreaks...some loves still live on;
New friends oft remembered long after we're gone.
   We're up early in the morning, up late at night,
   Talking and laughing...our "carryin' ons" are a fright!

Top bunks and bottom bunks...garb everywhere,
Folks bathing and primping and combing their hair,
   Gals laughing and giggling...boys spraying shave foam,
   Very few getting home sick and thinking about home.

Cutoffs, blue jeans and dress clothes, too,
Toothpaste, deodorant, soap and shampoo;
 Our rooms and housekeeping are a definite disgrace,
 Clothes, shoes and undies all over the place;

Stinking socks, dirty clothes, full of sweat and dust,
A clean change for tonight is a definite must!
 And the food...it's delicious...well, mostly that's true
 'Cause sometimes it's beans... and sometimes it's stew.

We have nurses and doctors and safety patrol;
Some children, and adults, and a few that are old.
 There's the chapel, tabernacle...and perspiration, galore,
 Yes, there's all of these things but much, much more;

Good preaching, good singing, attendance a must,
Hard benches, soft pillows...and short sermons...a plus!
 But the spirit of the God also comes to this place
 And many hurting youth meet Him face to face.

Many souls are rescued from the depths of despair
By placing their lives in the Dear Savior's care;
 New life blossoms forth, the old passing away,
 New lives trusting Him for each step of the way.

We're never the same when we trust in His Grace
Which is offered so freely at this special place.
 Many great things have happened, but the greatest to me
 Is when He touches a soul and He sets it free.

I know there's no magic in these rocks and these trees
But a miracle happens when we fall on our knees.
 And like the Holy of Holies in God's special way,
 His Spirit descends on this place every day.

We would all be better if the whole human race
Could experience Falls Creek...this extraordinary Place!

FOR GOD SO LOVED THE WORLD
A Song

For God so loved the world that He gave His only Son,
For God so loved the world that He gave His only Son,
For God so loved the world that He gave His only Son,
     Would you lay down your life for a friend?
Would you lay down your life for a friend,
Would you lay down your life for a friend,
     God so loved the world that He gave His only Son,
Would you lay down your life for a friend?

Do you love one another as Jesus loved you,
Do you love one another as Jesus loved you,
Do you love one another as Jesus loved you,
     Would you lay down your life for a friend?
Would you lay down your life for a friend,
Would you lay down your life for a friend,
     Do you love one another as Jesus loved you,
Would you lay down your life for a friend?

Have you opened your heart and let the Savior in,
Have you opened your heart and let the Savior in,
Have you opened your heart and let the Savior in,
     Jesus laid down His life for you,
Jesus laid down His life for you,
Jesus laid down His life for you, my friend,
     Have you opened your heart and let the savior in?
Jesus laid down His life for you.

FORKS IN THE ROAD -"Defining Moments"

I guess most people wonder who they are,
How they managed to arrive at this place,
Some are thankful and proud of the person they are...
But some are filled with shame and disgrace.

    Well, if we take a look back across the years
    Perhaps we can understand why,
    There are defining moments in everyone's life
    That we must live with until we die.

Perhaps there was a moment at an early age
When you chose whom your friends would be,
How you would live your life and what you'd do,
And since that time you have never been free.

    And other "forks in the road" all require a choice
    Whether education, occupation, maybe fame;
    What about drinking, gambling, or the mate you chose,
    Perhaps wrong choices have led to your shame.

And as the flow of our rivers that travel either East or West
Are determined by the great Continental Divide,
The decision we make at each defining moment
Will determine life's direction...and only you can decide.

    Whether it's the rivers that flow always downward,
    And grow ever larger as they rush on their way,
    Our lives can be caught in sin's vast current...
    But God will rescue and save you today.

Did you choose the wrong way at the "forks" in your life?
Are you traveling upon the wrong road?
If you're lost and bruised and hurting today
God is willing to lift your heavy load.

    In spite of bad choices, and sins and failures,
    God is ready to rescue, redeem and forgive,
    If you're ready to repent, to trust only in Him
    Then you'll receive a life that only He can give.

FULL CIRCLE

Let's pause for a moment and travel back in our thoughts
To a time when we were a kid,
   And think about some of those childhood days
   And about things our parents did.

Did your parents try hard to control your life
And stick their nose in most everything?
   Like, "Who was that calling you late last night
   We both heard the telephone ring?

Now, don't forget your coat, you might catch cold,
And be sure you look both ways crossing the street;
   Did you take all your medicine and drink your juice,
   And please, be careful of what you eat!"

Well, time trudged on and we grew up a bit
To those 'grown-up' teenage years,
   But they were just as nosey as ever before
   And their advise kept burning our ears.

"Drive extra careful on those wet streets...
And check your seat belt twice;
   You'd better get home before it's dark,
   It's too dangerous if the rain turns to ice!"

Were parents as "yucky" and things really as bad
As it may have seemed back then;
   Were they really trying to control all our lives,
   Or stop us from seeing a friend?

You know, it's much easier now to look back and see
Just what they were trying to do;
   They were showing their interest, their love and concern
   For me, and yes, you...and you...and you.

Well, I grew up...fell in love...and soon married,
And raised a wonderful, fine family,
    But, Life is strange...so confusing...it's a PARADOX;
    It played an unexpected trick on me.

A few years later LIFE threw me a "curve,"
It was the "beatingest thing" I ever had,
    I became a new PARENT...NO, NOT TO A CHILD,
    But to my aging mother and dad!

Life turned around, the roles had reversed;
I now found myself giving advice,
    Like, "You'd better get home before it's dark,
    It's too dangerous if this rain turns to ice.

Don't forget your coat, you might catch cold,
And be sure you look both ways crossing the street.
    Did you take all your medicine and drink all your juice...
    And please be careful of what you eat!"

Yes, my parents became my children, "in a way"
And I became their dad,
    But, When all was "hashed out," and said and done,
    I know they were really glad.

It was sad at the end when Mom was alone,
And I would whisper, quite loud, in her ear,
    "Mom, I wish you'd quit talking about Dad like that,
    He's been gone well over a year."

But time has done a new number on me
And my life is really getting wild;
    It's done a FULL CIRCLE like you wouldn't believe...
    Now I'm becoming my own children's CHILD!

Life has turned again, the roles re-reversed,
My kids are now giving me advise,
   Like, "You'd better get home before it's dark,
   It's too dangerous if this rain turns to ice."

Don't forget your coat, you might catch cold,
And be sure you look both ways crossing the street;
   Did you take all your medicine and drink all your juice,
   And please, be careful of what you eat."

They visit more, now, and give important advise
Like, what Mom should be feeding the cat;
   And, be careful Dad, you'll strain your back,
   And, Mom...you shouldn't be doing that.

They call every night before bedtime
And I'm not really sure what for,
   But they always say, "Now you write this down...
   And be sure to lock your door."

One day they came and screamed at me...
And at first I was afraid,
   "Dad, please, can you turn your TV down a bit...
   And turn up your hearing aid?"

It all seems strange to some folks, I know,
But I think I finally understand,
   That LIFE has made a FULL CIRCLE on me...
   And now I need a helping hand.

But I worry a lot if I've been good enough to my kids,
And that thought cuts me through like a knife,
   'Cause soon now they'll choose that rest-home for me...
   Where I'll spend the rest of my LIFE!

FULL VALUE

As I walked down the street my eye caught a glimpse
  Of something blowing and rolling around.
I turned to the side and glanced at the "thing"
  Now lying still, upon the ground.

It was sort-of green...kind-of rolled in a ball,
  It was crumpled, and dirty, and worn;
I thought to myself, is it worth my time
  To rescue something so tattered and torn?

Well, I picked up the "thing" and shook it a bit
  And, slowly, unrolled my find...
And what I saw, as I stood there in awe,
  Nearly blew my unsuspecting mind!

T'was not an old dollar bill, as I supposed,
  All covered in muck and in grime,
But I could see, faintly, Ben Franklin's face...
  It was a HUNDRED...and still worth every dime!

No, It had not lost its value...not even one cent,
  In spite of its condition and abuse,
In spite of neglect, degradation, soil and filth,
  And all its damage, disarray and misuse.

Now, that HUNDRED-dollar bill reminds me of those
  Who are stained and marred by sin;
They are battered and scarred, they are tossed and torn
  And have no peace nor hope within.

But, like the HUNDRED-dollar bill, their life is still worth
  All it was ever intended to be;
CHRIST will remove every stain if they'll call on His Name,
  He'll make them new...cleanse and set them free.

We are prone, many times, to think some life too far,
  Beyond rescue, redemption, or repair...
But like this bill, though blemished, tarnished, defaced,
  With the LORD, their full value is STILL THERE!

70

GOD THE FATHER
Wisdom from God's Word

My son, to fear Me is a sign of true wisdom,
My commandments are a light for you to see,
My words are sweeter than the honeycomb,
My love and mercy extends to even thee.

My son, a wise son will make a glad father,
A gracious woman is a pearl of great price,
But many a soul has been devoured and defeated,
By not following my admonition and advice.

My son, always attend to my counsel and direction,
Follow my words of warning without delay,
Wine, women and song have slain many a man
When life's temptations have caused him to stray.

My son, all the ways of a man are before Me,
I see every intent and thought of the heart,
If you are on your way like the "ox to the slaughter,"
I beg you, depart! Depart! Depart!

My son, if you will receive and accept My petition,
And keep my laws and commandments with thee,
And incline thine ear to the truth I now give,
My wisdom and guidance will make you free.

My son, forget not My Word and instructions,
They lead to a good life and long happy days,
Trust always in Me with all thy heart,
So I may bless your walk and your ways.

71

GOD'S LOVE
A song

Christ's death was true expression of God's warm and tender love,
No greater gift could come our way from the Father, up above;
That love was manifested as He bore the bitter pain
But the one and only Son of God will never die again;

    He bore the pain...but not again,
    The one and only Son of God will never die again;
    He bore the pain...but not again,
    The one and only Son of God will never die again!

To think Christ left such riches for a sinner such as me,
To hang upon a cur-sed tree that day, on Calvary
And the One who came from heaven to be mocked and cursed by man,
Laid down His life...in sacrifice...but He will never die again!

    All was not loss...upon the cross,
    For the one and only Son of God will never die again;
    All was not loss...upon the cross,
    For the one and only Son of God will never die again!

Christ came to earth to die upon the cruel, rugged cross,
God gave His only Son for man. That gain was heaven's loss;
He conquered death, the grave and hell...gained victory over sin,
Now He lives and reigns forever...and He's coming back again;

    His work is done...the victory's won,
    The true and living Son of God is coming back again,
    His work is done...the victory's won,
    The true and living Son of God is coming back again!

GOD'S PERFECT PLAN
A song

In early spring the flowers raise their lovely heads
From a wintry grave that's been so dark and cold,
Like our Lord, all nature rises from the dead,
Another miracle of life our eyes behold.

When the sun shines down and summer breezes blow,
And the fields are ripe and full of golden grain,
Does a life of peace and love within you flow,
Or is your soul all burdened down with sin and pain?

Do dark shadows veil your life of autumn treasures;
Does all the beauty remain that you have known;
Is there pain or is there loss from earthly pleasures;
Have you reaped, abundantly, the seeds you've sown?

Like the cold and chilling touch of winter's finger,
Death comes knocking every day at someone's door,
As you ponder over o're the memories that linger
Do you think about your deeds laid up in store?

Is it springtime in your life, is it summer, is it fall,
Is it wintertime and all seems cold and dead,
Is there joy or is there sorrow from the past that you recall,
Do you tremble from uncertainties ahead?

When the Reaper gathers in the fruits of harvest,
And the Blessed gather over on that shore,
Will your journey lead you to that land of perfect rest
Where the Saints will praise His name forevermore?

HEALED

There was a time in my life not so long ago,
A time of terrible, terrible distress;
   I was filled with fear;
   I was filled with pain,
My life was a horrible mess.

My mind was in torment, my body so frail,
My emotions so fragile and weak;
   I could hardly walk,
   I could hardly think,
And at times I would not even speak.

Now I thank you Lord for making me whole,
You're so merciful and true and kind,
   You have touched my life.
   You have touched my soul,
You have healed my body and mind.

HIDE AND SEEK

There's a little game we use to play
When I was just a kid;
I know that most of you recall
The things we often did.

We played a game called HIDE and SEEK.
And had a lot of fun,
And when our hiding place was found
We'd jump and scream and run.

Yes, those days were long ago
But at times we still act the same,
And though the years have passed us by
We often still play the game.

We like to HIDE from the world outside
Some of our God given traits;
It may be our weakness, or our strengths,
But it's something we think everyone hates.

And then we seek ways that are not our own,
And covet talents that we don't posses
To satisfy what we think others want...
But it always leads to pain and distress.

What a tragedy to live and never find
The person you were meant to be,
Because many times we hide our gifts
And seek things we want others to see.

It may be hard to find our "real self" inside...
The person that we really are,
But to masquerade as someone else
Will leave many and many a scar.

The "child" that's living inside of us
Has a longing to "come out and play"...
He longs to be free but you won't let him out,
Can't you hear him "crying," today

We may try to HIDE, abort or kill
The child we were born to be,
And seek or adopt some foreign way
That wasn't meant for you or me.

We each have a talent and temperament
That no other on earth may posses,
So accept and develop the "real person" you are
Don't HIDE AND SEEK something less.

God has provided for everyone
To be exactly as He wants us to be,
And really, you know, that's the only way
To be contented, happy and free.

So, when you find that key to "yourself and soul"
Guard it with unfeigned care,
For the enemy is watching and waiting for you...
He is always lurking somewhere.

HIS AMAZING GRACE
A Song

You ask a-bout the twink-le in my eye,
My friend-ly smile as I go pass-ing by,
This new and hap-py look upon my face,
It's all be-cause of His a-maz-ing Grace;

Chorus:
A-maz-ing grace that flowed from Cal-va-ry,
A-maz-ing grace that reached to e-ven me,
Lord bless the day you hung there in my place,
It's all be-cause of His a-maz-ing grace.

The lone-ly hours, those mo-ments of des-pair,
The hea-vy bur-dens were so hard to bear,
Lord, thank thee for that hal-lowed time and place,
Where I par-took of your a-maz-ing Grace;

The sin the pain, the load that I once bore,
The guilt the shame can con-quer me no more,
Lord, thank thee for that hal-lowed time and place
Where I par-took of Your a-maz-ing grace:

And now my world looks bright-er every day,
There's work to do and some kind word to say,
You give me strength to run and keep the pace,
I's all be-cause of His a-maz-ing grace.

HIS AMAZING GRACE

William O. Swain

William O. Swain
arr Bill Woolever

HOW DO YOU LOOK AT DEATH?

To most, the time of departing, when our loved ones slip away
Is a time of loss and sadness...but there is no other way.
It may be hard to leave this life and enter the one we await next,
But for God's child it will bring peace and joy, let's take a look in His text.

    God says, to be absent from the body is to be present with the Lord,
    2 Corinthians 5, verse 8, says so right there in His Word.
    Paul had a yearning; while here on earth, he desired to leave this life,
    And be with Christ, and leave behind, this world of hate and strife.

So, do you believe the scriptures, you can take it for what it is worth,
God says in Ecclesiastes 7, verse 1, the day of death is better than one's birth.
Do you look at death as God's Word says; how could this ever be so?
If there is truly a possible way, perhaps you will want to know.

    Well, in heaven there are no more partings, no heartaches, no more pain;
    Only joy, rejoicing and happiness; nothing sad, unclean or profane.
    No more doubts, dreads, departures, no more thieves, criminals nor fears,
    Only the upright, pure, Holy, who worship God through countless years.

No more wars, conflicts, confusion, nor those with hatred and evil ways,
Only the good, the clean and just, who will sing praises through endless days.
No more sorrow, suffering nor chastening, no more trials, agony nor night,
Only the redeemed live in this Holy Place, no more darkness, He is the Light.

    No more diseases, discomforts, disgraces, no more enemies, sin nor crime,
    Just those washed in the blood of the Lamb...only eternity...no more time.
    It is appointed unto man once to die, and after this the judgment day,
    The only escape of physical death is if Christ returns and takes us away.

Come out from among them and be separate, nothing of this world survives,
For by grace are we saved, through faith, if we're to live true Christian lives.
Yes, Jesus our Savior, deliverer, redeemer, only He can forgive and save,
He gives victory over Satan, sin, shame, and over death, hell and the grave.

ILLUSIONS OF LIFE

The race is not always to the swiftest
Nor the battle to the mightiest man;
Remember little David and Goliath?
Explain that to me if you can.

And remember the story of Daniel,
How they threw him into the lion's den;
Old Nebuchadnezzar and all his gang;
Oh, those wicked, wicked men!

But an unseen force was with him,
One that men of the world cannot see;
It was God and His mighty power
That set old Daniel free.

And Samson was a mighty warrior
'Til he forgot what he already knew,
That if he messed around with a woman,
The old devil is gonna' get you.

Beauty is sometimes deceiving
And strength may sometimes be a curse,
So, let us look to the Lord for wisdom
So we'll turn our better instead of worse!

IN GOD'S HANDS

If we believe in our hearts God raised Jesus from the dead
And if we will admit and confess our guilt and sin,
God will forgive us and accept us as His child;
That's when our new life with Him will begin.

What about this new birth, becoming a child of God,
Is there something or someone we can consult?
Yes, the Bible tells us we are saved by grace through faith;
Good works are not the reason...but the result.

Jesus said, "My sheep hear my voice and I know them.
My Father which gave them to me is greater than all.
I give unto them eternal life and they shall never perish."
So much more truth is contained in the writings of Paul.

But there is a question that comes to many a heart,
And I think it is wise to give consideration;
If a child of God strays from the Lord and sins...
What will happen...will he loose his deliverance and salvation?

Well, let's look in God's word and see what we can see,
I am sure the Lord's Holy Word will give light.
In Rev. 3 Jesus says, "As many as I love I rebuke and chasten,"
That's because He wants to correct us so we'll obey what is right.

Now why would He correct one who wasn't His child?
He knows no one lives a perfect and sinless life:
That's why in Luke 11:14 He tells us that every time we pray
To ask forgiveness for our trespasses, acts of sin and strife.

Jesus said not everyone who calls me lord will enter heaven.
If we trust in our own good works and righteousness
At the judgment He will say, "Depart from Me. I never knew you,
It's because of your lack of faith in Me, and your foolishness."

To enter a blood relation with those of our kin
We must certainly and definitely have a physical birth;
And so it is, to enter our Heavenly Father's family,
We must actually have a spiritual birth here on earth.

Once we're born into a family while here on this earth
Our relation to them may be filled with denial and scorn.
We may change our name and spurn and reject them
But there is absolutely, positively no way to be unborn!

Once we're a blood bought, born again child of God,
There is something in John 10 Jesus wants us to understand;
As in life, there is nothing you can do to be unborn,
Jesus tells us that no one can pluck us out of His Father's Hand.

IN THE DARKNESS

I don't know about you but I do love to drive...
That is, I love to drive in the day, not the night,
Because I love to see the mountains and countryside,
But in the darkness their beauty fades out of sight.

In the black of the darkness I can't see a single thing,
At times, faintly, I see something in front of my face,
But what a difference when the sun shines bright
We can see God's beauty and wonders all over the place.

But there are times we must travel in the darkness,
To do so we turn on the lights of our car,
No, we can't see all the sights and the beauty around
In fact, we can only see directly ahead, and not very far.

Perhaps we can see only fifty yards, or a little more,
And nothing is visible, all around us is darkness instead,
But you know, as we move along in the light we do have
The darkness is lightened as the light moves on ahead.

We don't have to see a hundred miles down the road
Or even a mile, or half a mile, or very far
To travel all night, perhaps many hundreds of miles,
If we move along in the light we have from the car.

And so it is in our lives, we can't see tomorrow,
And many times we don't even know about today,
But if we travel in the light that God gives us
He will guide and protect us, and direct us all the way.

And failing to move forward in the light we have
Has caused the failure in many, many lives.
You know, we really just live one day at a time;
Yesterday is gone forever...and tomorrow never arrives.

IT'S ONLY MAKE-BELIEVE

I heard this story from an old, old man
And I'll repeat it as he recalls:
Years ago, he said, that a daredevil man
Stretched a tight-wire across Niagara Falls.

    And then with great skill, and with pole in hand,
    He stepped, calmly, out on the wire;
    He walked back and forth and danced a little jig
    As all watched for what else might transpire.

He then placed a wheelbarrow on the tightly stretched wire
And slowly pushed it across and back;
Upon his return almost everyone cheered...
But this one fellow made a wisecrack.

    I have a hundred pound sack of potatoes out here
    In the back of my old Ford van;
    If you'll put them in and push 'em across
    I'll say you are "quite a man."

"I'll accept your challenge," he responded with glee,
And a murmur raced through the crowd.
As soon as the cargo was loaded in place
The cheers from the people grew loud.

    Then the vast crowd grew silent as the man took his stance,
    And with each handlebar firmly grasp,
    He slowly moved forward, one step at a time...
    Just one mistake could be his last.

But with impeccable skill he crossed over and back
To the shouts and cheers of the throng;
Never before had these folk had such a thrill
Nor seen daring and courage so strong!

The crowd went wild with tumultuous applause
    And with "whooping and hollers" and praise,
    But a few moments later the crowd grew quiet
    As his hand began, slowly, to raise.

"How many believe I can take from this crowd
One of you, here, this very day,
And push you across and back again...
Do you believe it...What do you say?"

    I believe it! I believe it! One could hear the replies
    Amidst the clamorous shouts of the crowd;
    Then, once again, there was silence as the man raised his hand
    And spoke clearly and forcefully and loud;

"You all say you believe I can take one across;
Who is the one that will take that ride?...
Well, I'm ready to go...Are you ready to go...
Who is the one that will step to my side?"

    The silence was chilling, then whispers arose,
    But not one stepped forth from the throng.
    "Where's the one that is willing? You all say you believe...
    Now don't tell me my hopes are all wrong!"

"But no one was willing," the old man said to me,
"Not one came forth for the ride.
One's belief in the head is not really belief
Until the heart is "standing beside!"

    What you have is one mixed-up muddled affair
    That's rolling around in your head...
    Because it says, very plainly, in the Word of God
    That faith, or belief, without works is dead.

Consent...Reliance...Submission...Compliance
Are the things true belief will achieve;
Belief, without action, is like form without life...
It's NOT REAL! It's only MAKE_BELIEVE!

IT'S UP TO YOU

What do you do when you're with a crowd?
Do you refuse...or go along
With something they expect you to
Even though you know it's wrong.

It's hard to walk the "narrow path"
When your friends don't understand,
And they poke a little fun at you
And they brand you with "that brand."

Before you make your final choice,
Let me say a word to you...
So many of those "little things"
Are impossible to undo!

You always reap whatever you sow
As sure as the setting of sun,
And most of the things you just "happen" to do
Can never be undone.

You can rant and rave and cry and wish
That you could go back, as some say,
To a time and a place where they made their choice,
Things would be different today!

Oh, how it hurts to stand alone.
When it's you who must face the test,
It makes you feel like your disowned
To be different from the rest.

But you really have a special Friend
Who is standing by your side.
He stood, alone, for you, one day,
He suffered, bled...and died.

He loved you more than life, itself,
He would not "bend the knee"
Though, while He walked this path of life,
He was tempted just as we.

And now He waits to comfort you
And always be your guide,
He will not force...He wants to lead...
But it is you who must decide!

JUST A SPARK

The wind swept across the prairie,
The fire raced out of control,
The flames grew hotter and hotter,
Like the burning within my soul.

I hadn't set fire to the prairie
That night out in the dark,
I only wanted a very small glimmer,
So I set just one...little spark.

But the mighty, raging inferno
Had grown from that tiny blaze,
Into unbelievable devastation
That now had lasted for days.

If I had known the eventual outcome...
If I could change my dreadful mistake...
Oh, I'd give anything to turn back the clock
And erase all the pain and heartache!

Could I go back to a time and a moment
And recall that fateful day,
I could easily have put out the fire
And stopped all the careless "horseplay."

It all started from one little flicker,
Lighted without forethought or care,
Much like the things in so many lives
That we oft times do so unaware.

Let's examine our walk down life's pathway,
Count the cost of the two different ways,
Then determine, for our lifetime remaining,
To follow Jesus the rest of our days!

LEARN, TURN, OR BURN

Sometimes you hear a very special speaker or preacher
Whose message you just cannot forget;
You're not sure if it's his subject or unusual outline,
And you still haven't figured it out yet.

   Many colorful preachers have a very unique ability
   To interest you and get their message across,
   Whether it's about loving...or living...or hypocrites,
   Or little children...or Jesus hanging on the cross.

One such message I'll make an attempt to relate,
It's about the prodigal son's life of rebellion and strife;
His days of disobedience were lived out in three different stages,
They were Madness...Sadness...and Gladness, in his life.

   In his MADNESS he rambled...he scrambled...and gambled;
   I'm not sure of all the other things he did;
   At first he thought he was happy living the "high life"
   While doing the things he should have forbid.

In his SADNESS he lost everything he had, or held dear;
He lost his togs...he went to the dogs...and ate with the hogs.
I'm not sure of what all he may eaten to survive
But with the husks he may have had the legs of some frogs.

   In his GLADNESS, after he repented and came home
   He wore the seal...he did the reel...he ate the veal;
   His father forgave him and restored his full fellowship,
   Yes, forgiveness and justification by his father was real.

The conclusion of the matter is very simple and plain;
Our Heavenly Father desires and welcomes our return,
But the decision is up to us, we must make the choice.
You must choose one...either LEARN and TURN...or BURN!

LIFE

Have you ever been in trials and storms of life,
Like the tornados that sweep across our land?
Most everything in their path is damaged or destroyed,
Hardly anything will survive and stand.

Usually, though, many things are eventually rebuilt
In spite of the destruction, the turmoil and loss,
And most things turn out better than the old
Even though there was great hardship and cost.

And even in our life, like the Hebrew nation,
Who suffered many trials, slavery and pain,
God used their "Red Sea" experience to prove
He was with them through their fears, once again.

He had not promised to remove the "Red Sea."
But to be with them and see them through,
And when you pass through the "troubled waters"
Remember His word, "I will be with you."

He delivered them from Pharaoh's army,
He made the "death angel" pass over the eldest son,
He caused their captors to give them abundance,
And that was not something He had previously done.

In our life God uses storms and "Red Sea" experiences,
Many hardships, many trials, many harms,
To prove He is ready, willing and able
To be with, and strengthen, us through the storms.

Roots of plants and trees mature more in the tempest,
The experts and horticulturist tell us so,
Storms and "Red Sea" experiences are designed by God,
They are needed and used by God to make us grow.

LIFE-CHANGING DECISIONS

There's some strange questions we face in life
As we think about from whence we came,
We didn't get to choose the sex we are
And we didn't get to choose our name.

    We didn't get to choose the nationality of our birth
    Or the place in which we were raised,
    We didn't get to choose the parents we have,
    But do you love them and give them praise?

Most parents do try to do what is right
And try to do what they think is best,
But many fall short in this important task
And fail, miserably, in passing the test.

    To be a good parent when did it all start,
    At marriage, or when you bought that first baby bed;
    Or did the things you learned in your youthful years
    Keep your thinking right and clear in your head?

Did you think in your youth that the "seeds" you sowed
Would some day be part of what determined you life?
The "seeds" that you sow, whether good or bad
Will, someday, bring joy ... or strife.

    Even a young child is known by what he does,
    Whether he is a "rebel" or a "normal" child:
    No, you can't live perfect but if attitude is right
    You'll make good decisions and not run "wild."

Do you want your children to point their finger at you
And say, "You're the reason I'm in this mess,"
Or, put their arms around you and hug you tight
And say, "Mom and dad, my life is really blessed."

    You must start at an early age to make decisions,
    In youthful years, or as a mother and dad.
    Daniel purposed in his heart at an early age;
    And young Joseph was the best ruler Egypt ever had.

Most of the wrong things you just "happen" to do
Might be forgiven, but they can never be undone;
So seek God's directions and answers to life,
He will direct and forgive. He is the merciful One.

    Hide the Word of God in your heart when young,
    It'll give direction and keep you from sin and shame,
    And whether young, or old, it will bless your soul,
    And you'll praise and thank that Holy Name!

LIFE'S GARDEN

There's a basic truth in this world of ours
That every young, and old person needs to know;
As strange as it may seem to some of us...
We actually reap what so ever we sow.

You can plant a very tiny grain of corn
And it will reproduce several hundred fold;
You can plant a pecan and when the tree has matured
It will reproduce thousands and thousands untold.

And it won't reproduce for only one year
But it will reproduce for your entire lifetime, maybe more;
And it's the same in our life of the seeds that we sow...
Is that what you're expecting and looking for?

It's wise to start at a very early age...
And especially in your teenage years
To think about all the things we do, or don't do;
Will they bring us joy, and peace...or fears?

Some of the foolish childhood things we do
May not lead us or cause us to go astray,
But some of the seeds we sow, the things we do
Will cause us to remember...and "regret the day."

The Bible says a wise son will make a glad father,
And even a little child is known by every deed,
So to make the right decisions in this life of ours,
Instructions from God's word is what we need.

The young Hebrew, Daniel, purposed in his heart
That he would not sin against God,
And Joseph fled the temptation of the Captain's wife;
I know some may think that was mighty odd.

Good seeds can be sown as well as the bad
In life's garden that will bring a happy life;
It's so much better when we decide today
To sow seeds that will bring peace and joy...and not strife.

LIFE'S OCEAN

Have you ever been adrift on life's mighty "ocean"?
All alone, afraid, and not knowing what to do.
You don't know where you are or how you got there;
You just know the furious waves are about to drown you?

You've never been in such wretched misery before;
You're desperate and helpless in this darkness of night;
What you need more than anything else right now
Is for someone to rescue and give you light.

The Lord is that someone who is waiting to help,
That knows all about you and your pain and distress;
If you're willing to call on the name of the Lord
He will save you from your hour of fear and hopelessness.

Christ came to this world to be a sacrifice for sin;
God so loved the world He gave His only Son,
Not for His sin... but for your sin and mine;
He died, and rose again, now His work is done.

"Come unto Me", said He, "All ye that labor
And are heavy laden, and I will give you rest;
He is our great physician, burden bearer and Savior;
He is the only... the best... He passed the test.

LIFE'S PATHWAY

As I've walked along life's pathway
  And I've viewed Life's changing scenes,
From the cradle to the ending
  And life's in-betweens.

I have one thing more precious,
  Rising far above the rest,
It brings joy...sweet peace...contentment,
  As I face life's final test.

I'm acquainted with my Maker.
  Long ago I made amends,
And I have a home in heaven
  When My pilgrim journey ends.

The time now grows more precious
  As I walk along each day,
Because Jesus walks beside me;
  He's my light to guide the way!

LORD HELP US

A chilling thought raced through my mind
As I listened last night to the news;
You can agree with me like many I know
Or you cannot accept my view, and refuse.

Someone had killed a little dog. I know that is bad,
He has been arrested and is in jail, my friend told me.
A disgusting and loathsome feeling flooded my soul
As I realized how blind we are, we cannot see!

I certainly don't agree with what the man did
And I'm sure there aren't many who do,
But we allow hundreds of unborns to be murdered every day
And we make laws to protect those who do.

What has happened to our beliefs and convictions;
What kind of people have we now become
To allow these precious little lives to perish,
Like the wicked people who lived in the city of Sodom?

God will hold us accountable at the judgment
For sacrificing these lives for our pleasure;
Yes, I'm sure God's heart has ached many countless times
For these little babes who are a part of His Treasure.

LOVE

Many people say "love" is what makes the world go around,
It'll drive away your troubles, and wipe away your frown.
    It will make you think thoughts you never thought you would think,
    And dream crazy dreams though you can't sleep a wink.

What is "love"... Real "love"? You may want to ask me:
To most folks it's a thousand different things, that's easy to see?
    To some it's seeking pleasure, or satisfying a fleshly desire,
    Some "love" a quiet home life...some have a lust to rule an Empire.

What about sports, or gambling, a new car, or a nice home,
It may be money, fame, or a vacation... like taking a trip to Rome.
    Some "love" a great big, juicy steak, or perhaps a chocolate candy bar,
    Others "love" to drink their whisky...and some to smoke a big cigar.

Most people "love" their family, their children...and their mother and dad,
What about the opposite sex, is that the strongest desire you've ever had?
    Some folks say they've fallen in "love" and set a wedding date,
    But in a few years it's no longer "love"... their "love" has turned to hate.

Many folks don't realize the reason their marriage didn't succeed.
They try to blame it on the other, because of want, misdeed, or greed.
    Perhaps it was for security, or passion...or a multitude of things,
    And oh, the hurt, the pain, the suffering that a wrong decision brings!

You know, the thing that many call "love"... is not really "love" at all,
Because true "love" never fails, we read in the Corinthian Epistle of Paul.
    We must let God lead us to that "one", if our marriage is to succeed,
    He is the only One that truly knows...and He has promised He will lead.

We use the word "love" too loosely. Yes...I'm very sad to say,
So many times it's just a desire, or a craving, that will not go away.
    And many mistake the true meaning, and make a mistake at the start.
    True "love" is not an emotion; it's very real; it comes from the heart

Christ relation to His Church is a pattern...from each of us to the other,
And if this is not true in your married life you're in for trouble, my brother!
    If your relation to your spouse is a peaceful and happy one,
    You are one of the fortunate, blessed souls living under the sun!

MY BIRTH

There was a man I knew when I grew up
Who was rich in fortune and fame;
I'll not tell you where he lived, you would probably know who,
And I'll not mention his name.

He had a son, who at first, was my best friend
Through childhood and into our teens,
But as he grew toward manhood his nature changed,
And he would use almost any means,

To get his own way... and to get what he wanted,
He would cheat and steal and lie;
He had no love nor respect for his dear Dad
And I could never understand why..

As I grew older I worked for the man,
I labored from sun to sun ;
The man treated me with feelings and affection
And I wished I could have been his son.

I tried hard to please him and I know I did
Because he often told me so,
But my worth, compared to his, was Oh so meager...
It would have hardly made a "show."

I thought to myself, if I were his son,
Someday I would inherit his wealth;
But all my work and effort didn't make me his son...
It only helped ruin my good health.

I had been better to him than his own "flesh and blood"
But I wasn't born into the family fold.
So when the father died, his real birth son
Inherited all his wealth and gold.

In later years the son did repent
And came back to the families' good "grace,"
But why hadn't my toils and works and deeds
Moved me into a son's worth and place?

It's the same with our life and relation to the Lord,
We're not His by our own natural BIRTH...
But we must have a SPIRITUAL BIRTH to become His Son
While we live our life here on earth.

It may not seem right; it may not seem fair
To work all your life, and loose...
But God has a plan, it's by His Mercy and Grace...
Not by our Works. And you must choose!

It's not by our works of righteousness, our deeds or labor
While we live on this earthly sod,
But it's by Grace through Faith in His death and resurrection
That we're born into the family of God.

MY FRIEND

I have a really special Friend
Who lives very far away.
I rarely get to see him
But I know I will someday.

I like his name; it's Leo Pool
And Leo is a twin,
Next time I go to Seminole
I'll see my Friend again.

I know that his deformed body
Is not as straight and strong as mine,
But deep inside that feeble frame
Beats a heart that is strong and kind.

Many, many long years ago
When I was just a kid,
I'll never forget a certain day
Because of what he did.

It was on a Sunday evening
As we were gathered there,
At the Baptist Church in Bowlegs,
In a worship atmosphere.

The Spirit moved upon his heart
As the preacher spoke the Word,
And Leo crawled...upon his knees,
To accept Jesus as his Lord.

And to you who have strong, healthy bodies,
Who are able to work and play,
Will you do as much as this cripple man
And accept Jesus as Lord, Today?

MY VALUE SYSTEM

What about me, what do I value most
In this world I am living in?
   Well, a lot of things now come to mind
   And I hardly know where to begin.

There's my family, my home, my job and friends,
And my education counts a lot;
   My health, vacations, security and retirement,
   And I'm sure there are things I have forgot.

How do I determine my value system?
Well, I know a good place to start,
   Let's turn in the Bible to Matthew 6:33,
   And let's meditate, and open our heart.

These words are the value system Jesus gave to us,
And many find it very hard to do,
   "Seek first the kingdom of God," He said,
   "And all the important things will be given to you."

He feeds the fouls of the air. He grows the lilies,
They don't work or worry or complain,
   Yet Solomon in all of his riches and wisdom
   Found that his life had been spent in vain.

How can we check our own value system
To see if we're obeying God's word?
   I'll mention a few of His own inspired teachings,
   Perhaps some of these you have already heard.

He said, "Where your treasure is there will your heart be also."
Are we following the instructions in His Book;
   Does it surprise you for what you're spending your money
   When you review all of the checks in your book?

100

Are we spending it mostly on necessary things,
Or for our "wants" and pleasures and fun;
    What about our investment in God's Holy Kingdom,
    That's what counts when our "race is run."

Let's take a look at our calendar and schedule.
Isn't it amazing where all the time went?
    Jesus said that no man can serve two masters;
    Does it surprise you where most of your time is spent?

Are we laboring to lay up more treasures?
Or, are we trusting our God to provide.
    He told us not to worry about tomorrow
    Because He is able and willing to provide.

When I look in the mirror of Jesus' teachings
And see how short I come in trusting His Word,
    I now repent, and ask for strength and forgiveness,
    And seek the mercy of my Dear Lord.

OH, WHAT GLORY!
A song

From the depths of sin, Jesus took me in,
And (He) showered on me His blessings from above;
Jesus rescued me. Jesus set me free
And (He) filled my heart with joy and peace and love;
Now I praise Him every day,
For this new and different way,
For the wondrous love He showed,
For the crimson tide which flowed

Chorus:
Some day soon He'll come for me,
Oh what glory that will be,
Then, praise His name,
I'll live with Him E-ter-nally!

Jesus bled and died, He was crucified,
Jesus gave His life on rugged Cal-vary;
What an awful price, what a sacrifice
For the Son of God to give His life for me;
Now I owe Him all I own,
For the mercy He has shown,
For deliverance from sin,
For a new life now within,

Chorus:

Since He saved my soul, since He made me whole,
I'll live for Him and bravely take my stand,
I'll sing and shout, tell the world about
His saving grace, and spread the news through the land,
How they nailed Him to a tree,
How He bled and died for me,
How He rose and lives again,
How He cleanses from all sin,

ON ANGEL WINGS

Dedicated To Those Who Lost A Child In The Oklahoma City Bombing

You were such a sweet, sweetheart,
Always pleasant, always kind,
Friends and family know that you were
Sweet as anyone could find.

When you were just a wee, wee babe
Your mom and daddy used to hold
Their blessed gift from heaven
And watch your little life unfold.

We'd rock you in the rocking chair
And we would always keep
Your tiny head against our cheek
Until you'd fall asleep.

What a thrill to have our baby
Snuggled close against our breast,
Just to feel your faintest heartbeat
And to know you were at rest.

God knew we had a longing,
Something missing, something wrong,
And then He gave you to us...
Just in time, you came along!

Yes, you were such a precious darling,
As pure as heaven's morning dew,
Your parents were so very blessed
To have had a priceless child like you.

But now, so soon, the Master's called
For us to give you back to Him;
We know you'll find sweet joy and bliss
In His New Je-ru-sa-lem.

Like the fragile flowers of springtime
That grace the fields across the lands,
This precious, tender life of beauty
Now rests, in peace, in God's own hands.

Yes, we know you're now with Jesus,
Oh the comfort this thought brings,
He has borne you safely to Himself
On Angel Wings! On Angel Wings!

103

OPEN ARMS

Have you ever been in the prison house
Of despair and fear and gloom,
Without a ray of sunshine...
Only darkness filled the room?

And not a single soul to help you through
Your long and endless night;
What you longed for most in your lonely hours
Was just one ray of light.

Perhaps one glimmer would help you see
The step that lay ahead...
But your outlook seemed so hopeless
In your distress upon the bed.

Then someone came to see you,
They brought a cheerful smile,
They talked and touched and listened
And encouraged, all the while.

They gave a word of comfort
As you anguished o'er your load,
They shared the burdens that you bore
As you traveled your lonely road.

The pain, the hurt, the heartache
That one is called to bear
Somehow becomes more tranquil
When there are those who care.

And the one who cares the very most
Is our Heavenly Father above,
His arms are always open...
Reaching out to us, in love!

OUR SCHOOLMASTER

Do you remember that day when you first went to school,
It was new, and you probably didn't know what to expect,
But it didn't take long to find out the teacher's job,
She was there to encourage, instruct and...<u>correct.</u>

I know it's different now than when I first went to school,
A way, way, way back...eighty-five years ago,
The teacher had a big paddle about two feet long...
And she often used it on me, yes that's so.

You know, the Lord also chastens those He loves,
We shouldn't despise the chastening of the Lord;
His chastening yields peaceable fruits of righteousness
He tells us over and over in His Word.

God gave us the law, not that we could keep it,
But to show us how unrighteous we are;
The law was our schoolmaster to show us our need.
Not how close or near we are to keeping it...but how far.

The Lord says that if you are without chastisement,
You are not His son, you do not belong to Him;
He pleads with us to follow His words and directions,
They are Holy, we should believe and accept all of them.

OUR SPIRITUAL ANCESTORS

Have you ever thought about the ones before
Who presented God's truth to you?
I think it would be good to pause for a spell
And give them the honor that is due.
    Was it your mother or father or teacher or friend,
    Or some preacher on TV or the radio?
    Or someone else, or something someone wrote;
    We should give thanks, don't you think that is so?
Let's look back a little farther in our thoughts and mind,
And ask, "Who told the one who told you".
We may seek the answer and some may find out,
But many will never, never have a clue.
    How far back can you trace your spiritual lineage,
    Who brought the truth from that foreign shore;
    Did Columbus, or someone on the Mayflower ship,
    Or perhaps a soldier on a battleship of war?
How did God's word get here, from Israel to you,
To the place where you now reside?
It didn't come on a cloud, or a strong east wind,
Or drift over on a stormy ocean tide.
    No it didn't...It took many faithful, true witnesses
    From the time of Jesus Christ our Lord,
    Facing persecutions, afflictions and imprisonments,
    And trials, and torture, even the sword.
Some were carried away to a foreign land,
Some were burned alive at a stake,
Some were exiled and never heard from again,
All for the cause of our precious Lord's sake.
    What about the ill treatment in their own homeland,
    All those years before the Pilgrims ever came,
    Before our country and government were established;
    We'll probably never, never know their name.
But...in heaven we'll meet our spiritual ancestors
Who were faithful to pass on God's good news,
And aren't you thankful you accepted His salvation
When you were presented with the right to choose.

Our spiritual lineage goes back to God the Father
Through our Lord Jesus Christ His Son,
If we're born again we're joint heirs with Jesus,
And there is no other way...no, there is none.
Is Peter, Paul or John in your spiritual lineage?
In every age someone has had to be true,
What about through the days of the dark ages;
Do you know who your spiritual lineage passed through?
I'm going to mention something that may seem strange
But however weird or strange...it is true;
What if your father had never been born,
Or, what if he had never fathered you?
You wouldn't be here...you were never born,
Not in this world we now live in,
You wouldn't have any family, father or mother
Nor any ancestors... or in-laws... or any kin.
You would have no lineage... past, present or future,
You just didn't make the human list
Because you were never born to the human race...
There is no you...you never did exist.
We must be born into the spiritual family of God,
A spiritual birth is of absolute necessity,
But, we'll have no descendants to follow after us
If we're not a faithful witness...don't you see?
We must be willing to pass on God's invitation,
Or many in this life will never be told,
If we fail, we'll have no descendants in heaven,
And no sheep for the great Shepherd's fold.
God has commanded that we proclaim His Word,
While we are still living on this earth;
Your spiritual ancestors have never broken the chain
Or you would never have had a spiritual birth.

This is For Us Old Folks:

OUR TREASURES

What are the things we treasure so dear
  As the "Golden Years" come our way,
That fill our hearts and souls with joy;
  May we think on this question, today?

Is it houses or riches or fortune or fame,
  Or some great deed that we've done,
That means so much as the years roll on...
  And we near the "setting of sun?"

Perhaps it's a wedding...or Christmas day,
  A present, a picture, a book,
A place with a wealth of memories...
  Or a special trip that we took.

To some it's the family that's cherished the most,
  Their "pride and joy" never ends,
Grandsons and granddaughter keep coming along;
  To others it's "tried and true" friends.

Our health and security and peace of mind,
  These surely will be on our list,
Our country, our church, our freedom, our flag;
  Is there anything else that we've missed?

A tear stained letter, a faded flower,
  In a Bible that's been set aside,
A handclasp, a smile, a whispered word
  From a loved-one before they died.

We all have treasure that live in our hearts
  That we hold very sacred and dear,
May we thank Thee, Lord, for making it so,
  Every hour, every day, every year.

PATIENCE

Lord, I need help...can You hear me?
I don't have too much time to spare,
I've found myself in a real tight spot...
And folks say that You really care.

I need deliverance from a lot of troubles,
Or I need someone to see me through...
Folks say there is no one else, Lord,
I can depend on like I can You.

I don't really know how I arrived, Lord,
But I sure am in one big mess,
I can't wait much longer...believe me,
I'm in terrible, terrible distress!

Could we both make a deal...or a bargain?
There's a few things I'd rearrange...
Just as soon as my troubles are over
And I find time to make the change.

I've tried to be calm and collected,
And use reason...and self control,
But Lord, I can't hold out much longer...
This suspense is taking its toll.

Lord, I'm calling on You, can You hear me?
I'm counting on You, Lord, somehow,
Lord, I'm desperate for help...and patience...
Lord, please hurry and give it right now.

POWER

What would you say, what would you do,
If all the power were given you
   Over earth and sky and beast and race,
   To make this world a better place?

Would you change the seasons, change the times,
Fill everyone's pockets with dollars and dimes;
   Move all the mountains to the sea,
   Flood the deserts, or let them be.

Reverse the order of oceans and tides,
Strip all the forests where wild life hides,
   Outlaw poverty and all disease,
   Make dollar bills grow on all the trees;

Make everything beautiful, everything strong,
Make long nights short... the short days long,
   Make all the dark clouds go away,
   Do away with night...have only day;

Make different languages all the same,
Raise all the dead...heal all the lame?
   Since we don't control the power we lack
   We can't make one hair white or black.

So...the only thing left for us to do
Is be content our whole life through!

PORTALS OF GLORY

Tell me, my friend, exactly what must I do
To earn or gain the everlasting Portals of Glory.
I've heard many things, I've heard many ways,
After listening to story after story.

Some say you must earn your way by right living each day;
Others say you can't earn it, it's something you must receive.
Some think they know exactly, there's only one way,
While others really don't know what they believe.

You know there are many, many things both false, and true
In this old world we are living in;
If you'll just look around it won't take very long
To know it is full of transgressions and sinners and sin.

There is only one place we can find out exactly
What we must do to enter Heaven's gate,
So if you are sincere and honest, and really want to know
Let's find out before it's everlastingly too late.

Because we are sinners by birth, we are lost without hope,
Unless we accept the free gift of Salvation God has given.
When we open God's instructions to St. John, Jesus said,
"Except we're 'born again' we cannot even see God's heaven;"
.

There was no way we could earn or pay our own way,
That's why Jesus left Heaven and came to earth.
God gave His Son Jesus to die on the cross
So that us sinners could be forgiven and have a "new birth."

It is by God's Grace, through Faith, we are made Whole;
That is what Jesus calls "being born again."
God gives us a new nature when we believe with our heart
And His Holy Spirit now comes to live within.

By His Grace, through Faith, we can receive a New Nature.
I know to some this may sound a little odd,
But because Jesus paid the price for our sin and transgressions,
We can now become Spiritual Sons of the living God!

111

PRECIOUS TREASURES

Sometimes our dreams of life are full
    of treasures, rich and rare,
Then clouds of gloom and doubt arise
    And drown us in despair;

And in the darkness, with no light,
    As we trudge on our way,
We may forget that God, Himself,
    Made night before the day.

But let a little light shine in
    And our eyes begin to see,
And our ears begin to hear things
    That we never thought could be;

It may be just a simple sound
    That once escaped our ears;
The singing of a mocking...
    How it thrills our soul to hear.

Or, the music of a water falls,
    The rippling of a brook,
Bright colors of the rainbow
    In the flowers on which I look;

Their fragrance is a sweet perfume,
    Fit for a maiden, fair,
Stirred by a soft and gentle breeze
    Pervades the mountain air.

 I love to see a baby bird,
    Or the buzzing honeybees;
An eagle soaring high above,
    The squirrels play in the trees,

The graceful flocks of meadowlarks
    That rise and take their flights,
Majestic, rugged mountain peaks
    That rise to lofty heights.

And Oh, the beauty of the fields
   That down before me lies,
The golden rays of sunset
   As they race across the skies;

God's world of sight and sound posses
   PRECIOUS TREASURES to behold,
This wealth is worth, by far, more than
   The price of all its gold!

RELIGION

Tell me, what is religion? Are you religious?
Can religion mean different things to different folks?
Yes, to some it's obeying different laws and rules...
And to some it may be being pleasant and telling jokes.

Some religious people are honest and true,
While some control other people, and deceive.
Some have a strict list of acts and regulations...
While others don't really know what they believe.

You know, everyone is religious in one way or another,
Even if it's just living and doing what comes naturally...
But what really counts when we leave this old world
Is not religion at all ...don't you see?

The thing that truly counts when we leave this life
Is more important than just following someone's creed;
There are hundreds of religions in every land
But something far more than religion is what we need.

No money, no works, no rules we may obey or keep
Can purchase our salvation, nor our sin or sins erase;
We need True Christianity! We need Jesus Christ
If we are to live forever in that Heavenly Place!

Jesus said, "I am the way, the only way,
No one can come to the Father but by Me."
Just religion, just being religious is no help at all;
If religion is your hope, He will say, "Depart from Me."

How sad, how sad these words Depart from Me will be
When we've had our last chance to make a Right Choice,
But what a day of joy, happiness, and Thanksgiving
It will be when we join with all those who rejoice!

RICHES

What is your biggest and most important desire in life?
To have great riches, and world wide fame,
So that everyone in the whole wide world
Will know you by sight, and your name?

The Bible says the love of money is the root of all evil.
Does that sound to you far out, and very odd?
Money does have a use and a place in our lives
But for many, it's their ruin...it becomes their god.

We are to work hard in our life and earn our keep,
Provide for our family and help the needy, we are told,
But what if our only desire is for gain
And we deny God...and loose our own soul?

What if we gain the whole world and its riches
And indulge in every thing and pleasure we can find,
Someday, and perhaps sooner than we think
Death will come and we'll leave it all behind.

What about living your life in the hereafter,
You don't die...it's just your body that is dead;
The rich man died and was in torment in hell,
That's what the Bible in Luke 16:23 said.

But God sent His Son Jesus to provide us a way
So that we can become part of God's family;
It's by God's grace through faith in Jesus' sacrifice
That our sins are forgiven, and we're set free.

Jesus said it's very hard for they that trust in riches
To enter into the kingdom of our Lord God
Because they trust in riches instead of God's grace;
Do you believe it...or does that also sound very odd?

Can a camel go through the eye of a small needle?
"It's easier for that to happen," Jesus said,
"Than for a rich man to enter into the kingdom of God."
He must obey and get God's way straight in his head.

Jesus said by man's works and his way this is impossible,
But not with God, because of His love He had a plan,
He sent Jesus, His Son, to redeem our souls;
If you believe and trust Him, He'll save any man.

115

RIGHT OR WRONG

How, my friend, do you determine what is right or wrong;
Do you get your values from someone's popular song?
    How, I ask, do you determine what is wrong or right;
    Do you decide on your beliefs from what you dreamed last night?

Do you study in your school all of these important things,
Or just take what comes along, whatever fortune brings?
    Do you seek wisdom from the world, or follow a modern trend,
    Not knowing its beginning nor where it all may end?

Do you determine what is right by what others do,
Or how your friends may look at things, or how it prospers you?
    Is it by someone's roll of dice, or chances you may take,
    And not by wise decisions that you have failed to make?

Are your "truths" absolute...are they right...are they wrong...
Or is each circumstance different when you go along?
    Are your "truths" absolute...are they wrong...are they right...
    Or do they vary according to what you do tonight?

Is there some place to go to find the answer to this;
Can we be unmistakably sure, can we know, and not miss?
    YES, there is surely an answer and it's all in a book;
    Have you ever seen it, have you taken a look?

The GOOD BOOK will tell you, it's sent from above,
And its instructions and wisdom are bathed in GOD'S LOVE.
    If you're sincere and honest let me suggest what to do,
    Just read all of its pages, every single word is true.

There is no better place in all this world you can go...
If you're ABSOLUTELY sure that you REALLY want to know!

ROMANCE

Romance is something that makes the world go around.
It'll drive a way your troubles and wipe away your frown.
It'll make you think thoughts you never thought you would think
And dream crazy dreams though you can't sleep a wink.

When the "love bug" bites you ignore your best friends;
All waking hours are spent together and you hope it never ends.
You try to stretch out each moment and wish that time would stand still;
Your heart pounds and races...what a thrill...what a thrill!

You fantasize about tomorrow and anticipate what it may bring,
There is magic in your music and the songs that you sing.
It's like heaven to be together when everything is alright,
The sky seems much bluer and the sunshine more bright.

Time flies when you're romancing and drags when you're apart,
But just a glimpse or phone call will start a flutter in you heart.
Some couples favorite time is the sunny hours of day,
They find so many things to do: work, study, eat and play;

But some folks are different, whether wrong or right,
They don't relish the daytime, it's the dark, late hours of night.
I don't know that it matters whether nighttime or day,
It's more the things that you do and the things that you say.

It's the way that you think that will most help you through,
The intents of your heart and the desires you pursue.
Some "romantic relations" are nothing even close to love,
They're just fleshly fulfillments and things I will not speak of.

But God, up in heaven, has commanded that we live
A chaste and virtuous life until He chooses to give,
A mate whom He has chosen, and then we two can be one...
We can love and come together with the blessings of His Son.

And God has ordained that we live a pure, clean life
Before this coming together of a man and his wife.
A marriage relation of two people in love,
Who are right in God's sight is blessed from above!

SCARS

Years ago I was hurt in an accident
And my body was battered and torn,
And the anguish and pain that I suffered back then
Was more than I had ever borne.

At times I didn't think I would make it through,
Oh, I suffered in so may ways,
The nights were longer than I had ever known...
And Oh...those dark and dreary days.

Now my body has healed and I've recovered my health,
Yet some ugly scars remain,
But the thing that means the most to me
Is that I no longer suffer pain.

I once had to bathe and doctor the wounds
And treat all the scars with care,
But now they are healed and as good as new
And I hardly notice that they are there.

But the wounds to our feelings, emotions and heart
Don't always heal nearly as well,
And we suffer with pain for years and years,
More than some tongues can tell.

And we oft times reopen old scars of the heart,
We just can't let them be,
And we continually go back to that time and place
That was so painful to you, and me.

We may regress to a point where our emotional state
Is some mixed-up, muddled affair;
Sometimes we won't rise, sometimes we won't talk,
We won't bathe or comb our hair.

We arouse and awaken many old wounds
Many times, over and over again,
So unlike the scars on our fleshly frame,
Which we let heal...and suffer no pain.

We revive and rehash and relive many things
That should have a long time ceased to be,
By night and by day we won't let them heal...
And so our hearts can never be free.

So, let's come to the one, great Physician
Who offers healing, deliverance, release.
He is waiting to rescue and comfort.
His way brings joy, and freedom, and peace!

SEEING IS BELIEVING

Have you ever heard the saying that "seeing is believing"?
Well, that's a pretty common thing some folks say,
Especially by many who live in Missouri.
You've got to "show me" before I'll believe it's that way.

But there are many things more important than just seeing,
You don't have to see them to believe they are real;
If you'll give me a minute to mention a few of those
I believe you'll be convinced they are real...is that a deal?

Have you ever suffered great pain or sickness,
Have you ever hated,...or loved...or had fear,
Have you ever been lonely...hungry...or angry,
Have you ever experienced joy, or happiness, my dear?

And what about being cold...or out in the darkness?
If you answered "yes" to these I don't believe you're right
Because there is no such thing as cold...or darkness;
Cold is just the absence of heat...and darkness the absence of light.

And what about those other things I have mentioned?
I am sure you must believe they are real,
But you can't see, or show me one of those things;
They are things you must experience to know and to feel.

And so it is with accepting our Lord Jesus Christ,
If you'll just believe and put your faith in God's Son,
He'll open your "eyes" so you can "see" and know Him,
Then He'll say, "Welcome my child, well done."

We must have a spiritual birth to enter into God's family,
God's Holy Spirit will guide us all the way,
We don't have to see with our eyes to know Him,
He is as real as the breath we breathe today.

God is just the opposite of "seeing is believing."
Believe in Him and He'll make you able to see;
With outstretched arms He is waiting to receive you;
"Oh, don't delay, come unto Me," says He.

SET FREE

One of life's deepest mysteries, to some, I know, is
How we all could be born in sin,
With a human nature that is opposite to God's,
That dwells in our heart, within.

God made man, Himself, in His image, I believe,
And everything else that we see,
But something dreadful happened in the Garden of Eden
When man "ate" of the fruit of the tree.

But the tree was beautiful, much to be desired,
Its fruit good and pleasant to the eyes...
And man found out later after eating a bite
That it would also make one wise.

But the price that he paid for the wisdom he gained
When he disregarded the words that God said,
Put us all in debt, in bondage, disgrace,
And brought the curse that hangs over our head.

Man discovered his nakedness, his sin, his shame,
And he tried, hard, to hide his face,
But because of his disobedience to God's words that day
The curse of sin came to the whole human race.

But we weren't present back then so how could it be
That we're now born under the curse of sin...
And as Jesus said in John 3:3
That we must be born again?

It's hard to explain to some, I know,
But would you let me give it a try,
And tell you why Adam's failure in the garden that day
Is the reason Jesus had to die?

We say in our land we are all born free,
And where we live, work, and play, we have a voice,
But a few years ago the Negro man was a slave,
He had no right...no say...no choice...

Not because he had lied, misbehaved or killed,
Nor had he taken anything of great worth,
But his birth into slavery determined his fate...
He was a slave just because of his birth!

Before he was conceived... before he was born...
It was determined he would be a slave...
But his Deliverer came... and he was set FREE...
Just as our Savior came to save.

Like the slaves of old we're born under a curse,
Our human nature is under the curse of sin,
But our Redeemer has come...He will set us FREE...
If we'll only be "born again!"

A new Spiritual Birth will break the curse,
That's why Christ went to Calvary;
We are now a sinner...Saved by God's grace...
We are a slave who has been set FREE!

SEVEN STEPS DOWNWARD

Paul tells us in Philippians 2 the mind of Jesus Christ...
And if we searched the whole world we could never find
Another who though being equal with the Lord our God,
Would think it not robbery to humble Himself for all mankind.

But Jesus Christ made Himself of no reputation
And took upon Himself the likeness of man;
For 30 years He lived a simple life, He became a servant,
And that is when all of His troubles and trials began.

He came to the synagogue on the Sabbath in Nazareth
And stood up to read as was His custom to do,
From Isaiah He read, "The Spirit of the Lord is upon me
And He has anointed me to preach the gospel to you."

He closed the book, sat down, and spoke to the people,
"Today this scripture is fulfilled in you ears," he said.
But instead of rejoicing all were filled with hatred and wrath,
And they thrust Him out and tried to kill Him instead.

But the life of Christ proved all of His claims to be true,
He healed the sick and blind; raised the dead; forgave sin;
He said the natural man cannot please God; he needs a new birth
And that new birth is a spiritual life He gives within.

He was true to the Father in all of His trials and persecutions,
Even in His death on the cruel and rugged cross of Calvary;
He prayed Father deliver me, but not my will but Thine be done.
His death make possible God's gift of salvation for you and me.

Yes, he stepped down from His place and Glory with the Father,
To pay the price so our new life in Him could begin;
He stepped all the way from the throne, to a manger, to the cross;
Christ gave His life, His all to be the sacrifice for our sin.

It is by grace through faith that we receive His salvation,
Not by any good works of righteousness that we have done;
He paid it all, the full price by His death on the cross at Calvary,
By the shedding of the righteous blood of God's own Son.

SIGHTS AND SOUNDS

Is there silence and quiet in the wide open spaces,
Or on a mountain top when you're all alone,
Or deep in a forest or a lush, green meadow,
Or your bedroom where you may have gone?

What if I told you there's a world all around us
That most people can't hear or see;
Where words and sounds and sights abound
That is meant for both you and me.

Do you think you would know it if they were really there;
Do you think you would know it if it were true?
We may live a whole lifetime without knowing this fact
So I guess a word of explanation is due.

The next time you think all is peaceful and quiet
Just turn on your television screen
And you'll see and hear many sights and sounds
That you have never ever heard or seen.

We are not conscious of the truth of their presence
And unaware of what they may have to say,
But the airwaves are full of countless sounds and images,
They are all around us both night and day.

And there's a whole other world, a spiritual world,
The human soul cannot experience or see
Until we tune in to God's spiritual "channel"...
Just as sure as we have to tune our TV.

How can there be sounds and quiet at the very same time?
Friend, that's not a mystery to me;
To hear the voice of the Savior in those still, quiet hours,
Your heart must be cleansed and set free.

Yes, there's another world that's foreign to most:
A spiritual world where God reigns true;
He wants us to hear, He wants us to see,
That's why He died for me and for you.

Yes, that's why Christ came to earth, to be that "channel"
Even though some may think it's quite odd;
If we'll accept this truth He'll open the way
For us to be in tune with the "Spiritual channel" of God.

As the air waves must be changed or converted
For us to receive all of the sound and sight,
We must also be changed and transformed by Christ...
Who is the Way, the Truth and Light.

STICKS AND STONES

I've heard a saying quite a bit
And it really does alarm me,
That "sticks and stones may break my bones
But words can never harm me."

Well, I have a different point of view
From those other folks I've heard,
Because just as deadly as a gun
Is a harsh, ill-spoken word!

You can tear folks down, you can criticize,
You can break a tender heart,
You can guarantee a ruined life
To a child, before they start.

You can take your sticks and all of your stones
Or a razor strap, to the young,
And do far less damage to those little ones
Than a spiteful, condemning tongue.

And older folks can be just as touched,
And oft times feel faulted and shamed,
And hearts may be broken beyond repair
By someone whose tongue is untamed.

You may throw your stick and stones at them
'Til you injure their fleshly frame,
But the awesome thing that is most to be feared
Is the tongue that no man can tame!

Sticks may sometimes beat one's body blue
And it may be bruised by stones,
But the wounds of the spirit and soul hurt more
That the wounds to the flesh and bones.

Have you wounded today...or helped mend a heart
With the words you so freely gave?
Yes, words do shape and frame one's life
From the cradle to the grave!

STORM CLOUDS

There would be no flowers in springtime
If the storm clouds didn't roll,
But each one has a silver lining
Just to calm the troubled soul.

In this world there's lots of storm clouds,
Lots of heartaches...lots of woe,
But we know the Lord is with us...
In His Word He tells us so.

We may not know nor understand
The rhyme or reason for our fate,
But God will answer in His Own time,
We can be sure...He's never late!

THANKS FOR LIFE AND LIBERTY

Many times we get so involved we often fail to see
Those countless, precious things that mean so much to you and me.
  Some are just the simple things of life that we see from day to day,
  Like Daddy coming home from work...and the children hard at play.

Bill is shining on his car, Ginger's rolling up her hair;
It's her first date...stepping out tonight, out to the county fair.
  Sometimes we visit with our friends, sometimes we take a trip;
  Have you ever been to Disneyland and rode a rocket ship?

And how about the joy that each and every Christmas brings,
When we sing about the Christ Child and hear the song about three kings.
  I can't see into the future but I can read about the past,
  How many days were dark and hard and heartaches seemed to last

There were famines, floods and riots and unrest on every hand,
But at last the night was ended and light shined across the land.
  There was war, bloodshed, and death, fears without and fears within;
  But alas, the night was over and our hopes renewed again.

Yes, we think about the future of this land we dearly love;
For all the bounty and the blessings we must lift our hearts above.
  We owe so much to many folks that perhaps we'll never see,
  So, let's give thanks to the One above for this Land of LIBERTY!

THE ANSWER

Can you tell me why I came here?
Why my life had to begin?
Can you tell me what I'm doing
In a world that's full of sin?

Where lonely hearts are searching
For the love folks never gave;
Where so many ones are hurting...
From the cradle to the grave?

Surely something must have happened
That is hard for me to see;
Can I ever find life's answer...
Tell me, will it ever be?

I know the answer that you seek,
You need a kind word to be said,
For a friendly hand to reach out
And, gently, touch you on the head;

To tell you of the Savior's love,
Of His birth, His death, His grave,
How He became the Victor...
How He arose, your life to save.

In ages past... when time began,
God made the heavens and the earth;
He then breathed life into that clay...
And now... He gives you birth.

He will heal your hurt...and comfort,
Give you courage, day by day;
He'll take you in His outstretched arms
And be with you all the way!

THE ANT

Yesterday as soon as I came home
I had a big, unpleasant surprise,
A million ants were crawling inside my home,
Right there before my eyes.

I yelled at them, "You ants get out of here"
But even in spite of what they heard;
God made a vast difference between us and ants...
I know they never understood a word.

I wished I could have explained to them
The difference between ants and man,
But there is a great gulf, a chasm between us,
And if I'm truthful, I know I never can.

If I could I would have told them that,
Their rightful place is down in the sod...
But like the difference between the ants and man...
There's a separation between man and God.

That's a perfect picture of God's state with man,
After the creation, and Adam and Eve's sin,
There was a great separation, a gulf, a chasm,
But God knew how and where to begin.

God had a plan to bridge that distance,
A plan that would set us all free,
He would lower himself and come to this earth
So He could communicate with you and me.

We were so short of God's power and perfection,
His love, His Holiness, His glory!
If you don't know exactly what God planned to do,
Let me try to tell His story.

He planned to come to earth in human form...
In the form of His only begotten Son;
When He did come He explained to the people
That the Son and the Father were ONE.

He came to span the gulf between us,
To pay the price for sin we could not pay,
He proved by His many miracles and resurrection,
That He is the One, the only way.

We are saved by grace through the faith He gives,
It's the greatest gift you will ever receive!
If you have never made that all important decision,
Will you, just now, open your heart and believe?

THE BALANCING ACT

Our lives are full of losses and gains
And hopes and fears and dreams,
And it behooves us all to find balance in life
Or so to me it seems

    It's OK to shoot for the best you can do,
    That is surely, only right:
    So...whatever thy hand findeth to do,
    Do it with all of thy might!

But it's so easy sometimes to go overboard
And take something to the extremes;
When we'd be better off with just a few more
Of those so-called "in-betweens."

    Sometimes we're happy, sometimes we're sad,
    Sometimes we fear what's ahead,
    But if we keep, more often, on an even keel
    We'd be much better off...enough said.

There is a time for most every purpose,
And a season for most everything,
And the sooner we learn this one lesson,
The sooner our lives will get "in the swing!"

    Life is one, long continual adjustment
    In this world as long as we live.
    There are ups and downs and in and outs,
    And oft times too much attention we give

To many less important actions or things,
And it soon may become an obsession,
Then we work and worry, toil, sweat and slave
But we never really learn our lesson.

We give much of life to our weakness and fears
And neglect more significant things,
And we later bewail our failures and losses
And regret the disappointment it brings.

Let's redefine our goals and make changes,
And pursue the things that bring peace,
And we'll reap the harvest of a well-rounded life
That comes from contentment and release.

Hey, let's all stop and smell the "roses"
Along the path of our life today,
Whether we're traveling through the bright sunshine,
Or the skies are dark and gray.

The race isn't always to the swiftest
Nor the prize to the most talented man,
So, let's determine now, once and for all,
To find the most in life that we can.

Let's put the genuine, most important things
At the very top of our list,
And I think, real soon, we'll come to find
How much of life that we've MISSED!

THE BLESSED HOPE

How much work must I do to get to heaven;
How many good deeds must I do;
Do I have to do one at least every day;
And does everything I say have to be true?

Does it take many long years of effort,
Of clean living, good works, good deeds,
Like giving to charity and the community food bank,
And helping the poor with their needs.

My religion is very important to me
And I try hard to do my best;
But sometimes I wonder when My life is o're
If I've done enough to pass the test.

You say your religion is very important to you
And you're doing many good deeds every day,
Hoping it's enough to earn your way to heaven
When you come to the end of your way.

Well, my friend, I hope I can be of help to you,
May I give you both bad...and good news;
There's two ways that people seek to be justified,
There's Religion, and Christianity...and you must choose.

All Religions seek to gain heaven by doing good works,
But Christianity is different from all the rest;
The Bible says it's not by works of righteousness that we do,
Nothing we can do will pass the test.

Our righteousness is filthy rags in His sight,
That's why Jesus came to die on the cross,
He came to pay the price we could not pay;
If you're counting on your works, all is lost.

He came to give us a new life in Him,
He paid the ultimate price for our sin,
God's sends the Holy Spirit to dwell in our heart
When we repent, and are born again.

Yes, our new birth makes us a child of God,
Joint heirs with Jesus Christ our Lord;
We don't deserve it but by faith we receive it,
By His grace we are saved...that's His Word.

Just think, all the founders of every religion
Now lie dead somewhere in a grave,
But Jesus rose from the dead and is now in heaven,
Our faith in His grace is what will save.

We are His workmanship, created in Christ Jesus,
A new person, created now, to work for Him,
To spread the GOSPEL to all the world,
To proclaim the GOOD NEWS in every hymn.

Yes, our salvation is a gift from Almighty God,
If we could earn it by works we could boast,
God sent His Son Jesus to pay our sin debt,
Thank the Lord, I believe, that counts the most.

THE BYE AND BYE

I watched in awe the tumultuous crowd,
All the excitement, the yells and the cheers,
   And the two dozen men who were playing a game
   That had become their profession and careers.

Yes, chasing a pigskin all over the field
And colliding with everyone around;
   And no one at all seemed satisfied
   'Till half of them were knocked to the ground.

It was the "SUPER BOWL"... as it is dubiously named,
I suppose it's "SUPER" for much of mankind,
   But as I saw the vast throng that was gathered there
   These thoughts raced around in my mind.

I wondered how much money and effort was spent
By the thousands who were gathered there,
   For the gas and the food and the hotel rooms,
   Not to mention the tickets and airfare;

What about the millions and millions the players received,
And millions for preparation, security and a TV ad,
   What about the "illicit things" I'm sure that went on;
   I didn't know whether to be sad...or mad!

Now, I'm really not against sports, as such,
I played sports in school long years ago.
   But I'm thankful and grateful to the Good Lord above
   I wasn't good enough to play college or pro.

I played every down on both defense and offense
In High School, back in my "heyday."
    I played safety on defense and quarterback on offense,
    And on offense, in 1944, I called every play.

But for the "Super Bowl" event, the energy and effort spent,
And the money that many couldn't afford...
    Now this is the question that came to my mind...
    I wonder how many came to know the LORD???

Why spend your money for that which is not "bread"
And your labor for things which never satisfy?
    Isaiah 55:2 asks this question of us...
    We'll have to give God an answer "Bye and Bye!"

What if all of this time, money and effort spent
Had been use to praise and proclaim the LORD???
    I feel sure that many a new soul would be saved...
    And many lives reclaimed and restored.

What if every person involved in worldly entertainment
Would obey II Chronicles 7:14?
    I believe God would send the greatest revival
    This old sinful world has ever seen!

THE CROSS

On a hill far away stood an old rugged cross
The emblem of suffering and shame;
Jesus died on that cross, paid the supreme sacrifice,
Jesus Christ what a beautiful, wonderful name.

The old rugged cross is made up of two parts,
The upright post pointing to the heaven above;
The rugged crossbeam held His outstretched arms,
Symbolizing His reaching out to us in love.

Much like the cross our lives consist of two parts,
The vertical points to God, the horizontal to man;
We have a spiritual side and a human side,
It's been that way ever since time began.

God has a job now for us, His children, to do,
We have now become His "outstretched arms,"
We must reach out with the word to those in sin
So He can rescue them from all evils and harms.

God looks at things from a spiritual point of view,
But, we humans usually look at things in another,
If we fail to follow God's Word and teachings,
What a mess we get ourselves into..."Oh brother!"

"Like Moses lifted up the serpent, I must be lifted up,"
Jesus spoke this message to His followers and friends,
"For this very cause I came to rescue the lost,
And this is where my earthly journey now ends."

THE ETERNAL QUESTION

The soldier's thoughts were racing, wildly,
   He was searching for a clue,
For just one reason men must die
   For those they never knew!

Young men, torn away from home,
   Carried far across the sea,
Thrown into a breach between
   The enslaved...and the FREE.

He has gone and he has given
   The ETERNAL SACRIFICE...
For our land and for our FREEDOM
   He has paid the UTMOST PRICE!

Why must men face such disaster
   Standing on the side of RIGHT,
Isn't there a better answer
   Than to bleed...and die...and Fight?

Yes, there is a better answer,
   But 'till all men see the light
Much is asked...and much is given,
   We must pursue all that is RIGHT.

And until that day and hour
   We must pray...and take a stand,
We must pledge a NEW ALLEGIANCE
   Everywhere throughout OUR LAND!

THE GOLDEN RULE

True happiness is a treasure that few seem to find
In this world as we're passing through...
If instead of the rule you search for the gold,
Disappointment will come to you.

Why can't we choose, each and every day,
Only right...only good...only true,
And reject the things of the world that we know
Will bring pain to me and you?

There's something that happens in many a life,
Whether in you, or family, or friend
That causes us, sometimes, to do the thing
That will bring sorrow to us in the end.

"What is it," you ask, "Can you tell me
Why us human folks so misbehave;
Why we harm and hurt each other, at times,
From the cradle to the grave?"

Wouldn't we all be better in this world of ours
If we could just, somehow, understand
There are folks out there who are hurting so,
And lend a friendly and helping hand?

Is there anything in your own life today
That you know might bring pain or sorrow;
Won't you determine, today, to live life the way
So there'll be no pain or regrets tomorrow?

THE GREAT DIVIDE

While traveling high up in the Rockies
Over mountains that spread far and wide,
I came suddenly upon a road sign,
It read, THE CONTINENTAL DIVIDE.

It isn't always on the highest mountain
Where the line of THE GREAT DIVIDE lays,
But it's the point where our land is divided
Into paths that lead different ways.

Two drops of water may fall close together
On a mountain top, side by side,
And be swept into opposite oceans,
Their course determined by this GREAT DIVIDE.

The direction of a droplet of water
Might be altered on the mountain peak,
At this point which determines its direction,
By soft winds...or a bird and its beak.

But let a drop start its journey downward
And it doesn't take a "week and a day"
To see that it's well nigh impossible
To change its course to the opposite way.

And its flow travels faster and faster
And gains "company" every hour of the day,
Until a swift, mighty, rushing torrent
Flows over everything in its way.

Can you remember a point...or a moment,
At a GREAT DIVIDING LINE in your life
Which determined your course and direction...
Did it lead to calm waters...or strife?

Are you in one of life's raging torrents,
Or do your "waters" flow peaceful and still;
Do you long to change one of life's courses
But you can't make the stream flow uphill?

You're traveling "east" but you want to go "westward,"
You long to journey in the opposite way;
You never dreamed, in your wildest imagination,
You would end up where you are today!

You can't go back to that point of beginning,
Too much water has run under the bridge;
But may I give words of solace and comfort?
I would count it a real privilege.

Each tomorrow brings the dawn of a new day,
And in life, a NEW DIVIDE... and you may choose
To start your life on a different and new way...
Don't hesitate...don't delay... don't refuse!

THE HILL

Long ago on a hill called Mount Calvary,
Three men were condemned to die,
    By the most cruel and painful death ever known to man,
    It was to CRUCIFY!

When the nails were driven two cried out in pain,
But One never said a word,
    No screaming, no cursing, no blame from Him.
    No accusation from Him could be heard.

The three men were crucified together,
Possibly only eight or ten feet apart,
    But their reactions were far, far different,
    That was easy to see from the start.

The one on the left railed at Jesus,
"If you're the Christ come down and save us today,
    And save yourself, too, if you're the Messiah.
    I really don't want to die this way."

But the one on the right believed in Jesus
And rebuked the unbelieving thief.
    Jesus showed His Love and Mercy by forgiveness,
    And gave him peace and sweet relief.

When the thief asked Jesus to remember him,
Perhaps to his great surprise,
    Jesus promised they would be together,
    Yes, that very day in Paradise.

Two thieves and Jesus were crucified,
Probably the same distance apart:
    What caused one to revile and curse Jesus,
    While the other thief opened his heart?

Everyone has the same choice as the two thieves,
While we walk this earthly sod;
    We must believe and accept or refuse and reject,
    The one and only Son of God.

A blind man had asked Jesus to be given his sight,
And can't you imagine his great thrill,
    When Jesus stopped and spoke these words to him,
    "I will...I will...I will!"

Yes...The decision we make with our willing heart
Will determine our destiny.
    Will you...or won't you, trust Jesus Christ?
    He died on that cross for you and me.

THE LAW OF HARVEST

I saw a man sowing in his field, one day,
And I asked what, per chance, might it be;
And if he always reaped the same as he sowed?
"Just come by in harvest," said he.

"I've planted corn and potatoes, sown rye and wheat,
Some shallow, and some planted deep,
And whatever is sown by these hands of mine
Is exactly the thing I will reap."

That's a part of the law of harvest...
But the rest is as equally true,
Just one little seed, when it sprouts and grows,
Will multiply, untold times, unto you.

Years ago I planted just one little seed
And, you see that pecan tree out there?
Through the years I've reaped many a thousand fold
And, you know, it still continues to bear.

It's exactly the same in the course of time
As we travel along life's way,
The seeds that we sow, intended or not,
Will return a great harvest some day.

Sometimes we're o'er whelmed and we can't understand
Why we're crushed by the weight of some load,
And it doesn't seem right that such a harvest could come
From just one little seed that we sowed.

But the same is true of the good seed that we sow,
It may return many thousand fold
And continue to nourish and bless and increase
Throughout life...even when we are old.

So, let's take note of the law of harvest
And be careful in all that we do,
The seeds that we sow, whether good or bad,
Will return a great harvest to you!

145

THE MASK

I was invited to a party the other night
With people whom I thought I knew,
But when I arrived I was greatly surprised,
I recognized only one or two.

All of those present were wearing a mask,
Their intentions were to fool everyone;
After looking around I thought to myself,
"What a good job they all have done."

Their purpose was trickery, pretense, deception,
But they were only playing a game;
Then a thought pierced my heart as I realized
That many of us may be doing the same.

In this game of life as we face the world,
Sometimes with fear and dread,
We are afraid, or ashamed, of who we really are
So we put on a "mask" instead.

We want others not to see the true person we are
But whom we think they want us to be,
And we try to walk in someone's shoes
And live a life we want them to see.

Are you wearing a "mask", deceiving others...and yourself,
Do you really know who you are?
Have you spent all your life pretending to be...
Has your behavior really gone that far?

Is your life in a mold, unnatural to you
Are you wearing that "mask" on your face?
Is the life you are living not really you...
Is it something you would like to erase?

What about the "Real You", your feeling, your fears,
What about your "Real Personality"...
Do you long in your heart to be free and apart,
To be the person God meant you to be?

He was your master designer, life giver, supplier,
And His wisdom is far above man;
You are a unique individual, remarkable, original,
For a very special place in His plan.

It would be terrible, awful, tragic, horrible,
A great loss to God's plan, don't you see,
To live your entire life wearing a "mask"
And never know the person you were meant to be.

 We are all similar but different...each, one of a kind,
No one's exactly like you...but you,
But we must take off our "mask" and find who we really are
To do the special job only YOU can do!

It may be hard, harsh and very difficult,
When the pressures around us press in,
But let us face the issues and take off the "mask"
And start today, where you are, to begin.

Loose those shackles that bind, start "homeward" today,
Come "Home" from life's troubled "sea"...
Come "Home" to peace and comfort, and be your True "Self"...
Come "Home"...Come "Home" and be set free.

THE MIRROR

Early in the morning when you look in the mirror
At someone that positively can't be you;
You don't want anyone to see what you really look like,
So what in the world are you going to do?

Well, you try hard to cover the wrinkles and bumps;
Twist all of those straight hairs into a curl;
You paint and powder and shave and perfume
And hurriedly hustle yourself out into the world.

You really haven't changed anything about yourself,
You've only covered up flaws the mirror has shown;
But that's one purpose of the mirror, to show yourself
What only you and a very few others have known.

But there's another mirror that is far more important,
It will let us look past our physical sight;
It will show us, convict us, and lead us in the way
Of the things that God tells us are wrong or right.

When you look in the mirror of God's word He has given,
How do you see yourself as obeying His Word;
Have you confessed your sins, received His forgiveness,
Or do you just think they are silly words you have heard?

Do you see yourself as just as good as the rest?
Well, that may be true for many of mankind,
But to have the peace, love and joy, you are looking for...
If you'll come to Jesus...all of these things you will find!

Be as honest with yourself as when you looked in your mirror;
When you saw yourself in all your spiritual disarray;
If you'll be honest, and call on the Lord for salvation
He'll, forgive you...and you'll become His child today!

THE MYSTERY OF SPRING

Like Christ's awakening on resurrection morning,
From a dreary grave that was so dark and cold,
New life bursts forth...'tis God's miracle of springtime;
All nature rises as enraptured eyes behold.

Melting snow makes streams that echo sounds of music,
Rippling brooks send forth enchanting, sweet refrains,
Percussions rumble from the mighty, rolling thunder,
Rich meadowlands and fields drink in the rain.

Birds, all feathered in their bright and bold array,
Flutter, mate, and dart from tree to tree,
Shrilling chirps and songs and serenades of love
Cover the entire scale from "A" to "Z."

Such innate beauty in the life of every creature,
Such joy to witness what another day can bring,
Oh, the splendor and the grandeur and the wonder of it all...
Such utter magic...'tis the MYSTERY OF SPRING!

Is it Springtime in your life, is it Summer, is it Fall,
Is it Wintertime...and all seems cold and dead,
Is there joy or is there sorrow from the past that you recall?
Cheer up, my friend...there's glorious days ahead!

THE PROMISE LAND

What do we think when we say "The Promise Land?"
We're usually talking about heaven, aren't we?
But what about the Hebrew Children that God lead along
Through the hot desert and through the fearful Red Sea?

They wandered in the wilderness for forty long years
Because in spite of God's mercy, miracles and His love,
They never trusted, nor sought, nor wanted His will
From the wise and blessed heavenly Father up above.

The land they were seeking that God had promised,
They could have reached in a few days or two weeks,
But they were rebellious; they murmured; they didn't believe.
They didn't have the faith that a Holy God seeks.

Out of all of the able men who were numbered at Sinai...
How many of them made it into the promise land?
Only two, Joshua and Caleb, from those above twenty
Were led across the river Jordan by the Master's hand.

Yes, only two entered out of perhaps a half million;
What a chilling, a somber, and sobering thought:
When it's our time to enter our "Promise Land"
Will the Lord say we have done the things we ought?

And even back in Noah's day, even before Jesus came,
To die for us, to pay the price with His blood;
What a terrifying thought, all the people washed away,
Except the eight souls who were saved in the flood.

Jesus said straight is the way and narrow is the gate
And not everyone who calls me Lord will enter in;
We must believe with our heart in His death and resurrection
Because He paid the price we could not pay for our sin.

You know, it's not by works of righteousness that we do,
But it's by God's grace through faith that we are made whole;
God sent His only Son, Jesus Christ, to die on a cross;
Yes, He paid for our sin. He shed his blood to save our soul!

150

THE RAINBOW

As the sky began to darken
And the clouds began to roll,
The thunder and the lightening
Caused a fear within my soul.

The storm grew strong and violent,
Raging winds...torrential rain...
Boisterous forces beat upon me
Causing terror...grief and pain.

I had felt hurt and anguish
In other storms that I had known;
Not from winds and not from water...
But from seeds that I had sown.

When the floods of life o'er take us
And fierce storms rage in our soul;
When we're tossed and torn and beaten,
Drifting opposite from our goal;

Just keep Faith...the sky will lighten,
God will spare us, like He said;
LOOK, I see His blessed Rainbow
Shining brightly up ahead!

THE RECIPE

Can you come with me and travel back
   To a time when you were a kid,
And think about some of those by-gone days
   And the crazy things that you did?

Like, when Mother went into the kitchen
   To cook some cookies...or bake...
You would climb up in a kitchen chair
   And "help" her bake that cake.

You'd eat some sugar right out of a spoon,
   And put cocoa in your lip;
Taste butter and shortening and soda and salt,
   And drink extract, sip by sip.

What awful tastes! But wasn't it fun,
   And I never could quite understand
How Mom could mix them all just right
   And come out with something so grand;

Like a great big, delicious, chocolate cake,
   Or those cupcakes she made in a pan...
And how could such terrible tastes become
   One of the best tastes known to man

Tasting each by itself, apart from the whole,
   Had certainly been no delight,
But a "master" had taken each separate thing
   And measured and blended just right.

And so in our lives each and every thing
   That we may think so out of accord,
Will work together for our blessings and good
   To all those who love the Lord.

So let us take courage in times of trouble,
   And find peace in the midst of the storm,
Trust our MASTER to work His good pleasure
   And deliver our soul from all harm.

THE RECITATION

I was elated and thrilled to be quoting
The most famous Psalm of them all;
Many feel, that for elegance and beauty,
Psalms outranks the writings of Paul.

My presentation was stylish and faultless,
Precise expressions were the rule of the day,
Each word flowed at a peak of perfection,
My talents were definitely on display.

Many cheered, while others applauded,
I was exuberant...ecstatic...misty eyed;
With jubilation I acknowledged the honor,
I had spoken with eloquence and great pride!

Sometime later, per chance, I heard another
Quote the Psalm, as he stood in my place;
As he spoke the same words, with conviction,
A radiant smile slowly covered his face.

When the recitation was over and ended
No praise, nor applause did he seek;
The crowd sat in awe...and in silence...
A tear flowed down many a cheek.

I had delivered the Psalm, in perfection,
Perfect diction and expression of each phrase,
But, the other, in a meek and lowly manner,
Exuded humble adoration and praise.

I had spoken the Psalm of the Shepherd
With eloquence, with force and with grace,
But the other had met the Shepherd
And communed with Him face to face!

THE SAVIOR

The Savior waits
To comfort you
And always
Be your guide;
He will not force,
He want's to lead
But it is you
Who must decide!

THE SCRIPTURE

Have you ever thought about the Word of God
And considered the wisdom and truth it brings,
   But wondered why His blessed, inspired Holy "Writ"
   Spends much more time on a few certain things?

Let's think for a moment about all of God's creation;
That information is important, don't you think?
   But compared to all of the Bible's 1189 chapters,
   Let's see why God only gives it a little "wink".

The first 11 chapters of God's inspired Holy Scripture,
Cover all His creation and first 2000 years of mankind;
   If it takes the other 1178 to cover the next 2000 years
   There must be something important that we need to find.

What is so significant about those next 2000 years
That makes up the rest of the Holy Word of God;
   It must be of utmost importance, don't you think,
   Or do you think it is just something very odd?

Well, let's consult the One who gave us the scripture,
And perhaps we'll see what we really ought to see;
   Jesus told the eleven to search the scripture,
   "For they are they" He said, "Which testify of Me."

Now the only scriptures that were written at that time
Were the Prophets, the Psalms and the Law,
   When they realized the scriptures were all about Jesus
   They rejoiced, and their hearts were filled with awe.

Then Jesus led His disciples out as far as Bethany;
He raised His nail scared hands and blessed the eleven.
 "Stay in Jerusalem," He said, "Until endued with power,"
 Then Jesus slowly ascended to His Father in heaven.

The commercial world overemphasizes things like Christmas,
They've thrown Christ out and made it a worldly holiday,
 So have many churches and professing Christians,
 And to others, Christ is left out of everything, I'm sad to say.

The angels rejoiced when Jesus was born in Bethlehem,
But no one knows the actual date of Jesus' birth;
 And 2 of the 4 gospels about the life of Christ
 Don't even mention a word about His coming to earth.

The chapters in Matthew, Mark, Luke and John total of 89,
And only 4 relate His birth, and first 30 years of his life,
 But 85 chapters cover Jesus ministry and last three years,
 Amazingly, 27 chapters cover the last eight days of His life.

Yes, Jesus was born, and it's imperative He came to earth
But His life, His death and resurrection are the key,
 So let us study His Word and search the scriptures
 Because it's by His dying for us that we are now set free.

THE SIMPLE THINGS

How could Jesus death on a cross affect my life?
How could His blood wash away all my sin?
How could I become a real child of God?
How could my heart and life be changed within?

You know, Jesus uses the very simple things
And He never does have to apologize.
The simple things of Jesus is foolishness to many,
But this "foolishness" confounds the "mighty and wise."

You see, Jesus was incarnate, God in the flesh,
He created the world, and you, and me;
He proved Himself by rising from the dead,
That's why He has the power to set us free.

The cost was tremendous, but His plan so simple
That even a child shall not err therein,
But we must put faith in His death and resurrection,
Still, His simple plan is foolishness to those in sin.

But surely there is something that I must do
In order to earn, and deserve, this right.
No, It's not by works of righteousness that you do,
Just open your heart and believe, with all your might.

THE STUMBLING STONE

I was stumbling and staggering in the darkness of night,
Without a sense of direction, alone, affright.
I was lost, uncertain, on my desolate way
Without a light to guide this vessel of clay,

I was desperate, lonely, life's breezes were cold;
Waves of fear and despair were flooding my soul,
Then suddenly, ahead in the dark, dreary night,
Through tear filled eyes I saw a glimmer of light.

Someone was coming...I now could see,
Someone was coming...to rescue me
From my prison of darkness, from my night all alone,
To rescue ME...from my Stumbling Stone;

To show ME the way where my feet must tread,
To lighten my way just up ahead.
I now see beyond that STUMBLING STONE;
With Jesus my Savior, I am never alone!

THE TEACHER

It's really hard for many people to admit they're wrong
Or honestly look at or consider the other's point of view;
We don't want to admit that we might not be right...
I wonder if this might possibly be true about you?

    I know we're all different in personalities and traits'
    But many times this is not the real reason why
    It's so hard for us to even listen to the other side;
    And some will even hold their own view until they die.

There are those who never learn much in school or in life;
All they want is to argue and always have their own way,
But for every thing we do there will be a consequence
And sooner or later there is coming a judgment day.

    Numerous times consequences are very cruel and harsh,
    But for many this is the only teacher they ever "hear"...
    They never learn from those who have been there before
    And they struggle through life for many and many a year.

But there's one thing even more important than things in life,
It's the decision we've either made or not made about our soul!
Just pause now and think for a moment about your life hereafter,
Where will you go when God stands up and calls His Roll?

    The Bible says the wise "man" will take heed, listen and learn,
    But the fool will mock and not consider God's way...
    If you haven't learned that God's way leads to truth and life
    Will you admit your transgressions and trust Jesus today?

THE TEMPLE

The Temple is where God the Father resides,
In the Holy of Holies, the very most sacred place;
No one can enter, and they cannot even approach it,
But the High Priest, where he meets God face to face.

What would you do if you went to the Temple,
With Jesus Christ to worship our Father God?
You know, one time when Jesus went to the Temple
He was very angry, and drove the people out with His rod.

Yes, the temple of God is a very high and holy place,
And it demands our adoration, honor and reverence;
If you defame or show disregard to His Holy Temple,
You will do it at your very own costly expense.

Do you go or have you ever gone to God's Temple?
Do you know if there is one where you live?
If you really want to know and ready to find out,
How much would you be willing to give?

Well, let me tell you something that may surprise you;
There is a Temple nearer than you might think.
If you are a child of God your body is God's Temple;
Does that thrill you... or does it make your heart sink?

Paul tells us in the Bible our body is God's Temple;
Do you reverence it; keep it clean and pure?
Yes, our body is the Temple of the living God
And God demands reverence and respect, that's for sure!

Do you take it to wicked and ungodly places;
Do you fulfill immoral desires and sinful lusts;
Would you take Jesus with you every where you go,
Or would He condemn your choices in deep disgust?

God's is love... but the other side of love is justice;
Unless we're His child, His judgment day will spell doom:
It's a fearful thing to stand in judgment by the living God,
So cleanse your temple...make it sure...don't assume.

THE THORNCROWN CHAPEL

This wood and glass masterpiece at Eureka Springs, Arkansas was designed by award winning architect, E. Fay Jones. Mr. Jones was recently honored with a gold medal for Lifetime achievement from the American Institute of Architects, presented at the White House by President George Bush.

On a quiet, Ozark hillside
Amidst majestic Oaks and pines,
Stands the little Thorncrown Chapel
Where heart of God and man entwines.

This picturesque and unique splendor
Of heaven and earth in one accord,
Stately arrayed in natural grandeur,
Reflects the Glory of the Lord!

Such Holy calm and sweet communion
Overwhelms the soul with awe,
Turns one's thoughts and meditation
Toward the Babe the shepherds saw;

How, in like hills of yon Judea,
An obscure Baby born on earth
Became God's sacrifice for sin;
BEHOLD...it was His Virgin Birth!

Now, like our wondrous, glorious Savior
Who redeemed us from the fall,
Stands the little Thorncrown Chapel
To royally welcome one and all.

THE TRUTH SHALL MAKE YOU FREE

The poem starts as a conversation between two people:

It's so important that we study the Bible and learn of God's truth, and believe...
"Oh, you feel that just heartfelt sincerity will bring the goal which you hope to achieve?"
   "Well, I certainly insist in the freedom to determine, for myself, what is real
   And I believe that the truest religion is being honest to the way that we feel.

We must trust in our own strengths and wisdom in this life if we're going to win.
That is why I'm so zealous of good works; Oh, I make mistakes...but is that really sin?"
   "Well, let's open the Book of God's wisdom and take a look at what we can see;
   God has given us a special promise...He said, 'The Truth Shall Make You Free!'

We're not saved by our own works of righteousness nor anything else that we've done
But by the washing of regeneration, by JESUS CHRIST...GOD'S Only SON!"
   "Well, I have faith in myself and my abilities, and I can see no reason nor rhyme
   That it's wrong to pursue my own judgment; Really, now...is that such a big crime?"

"It's not by might, nor power, but MY SPIRIT, saith the Blessed LORD, in HIS BOOK;
So, if you think you're 'Something' when you're 'Nothing'...you'd better stop and have yourself
another look."
   "I didn't say that my life is all perfect, but I'm proud of the things that I've done,
   And I sincerely believe that I'm worthy...Man, I labor from sun to sun!"

"All have sinned and come short of God's glory."   "But I do all I can every day-
My good works count a lot...believe me."   "But there is, JESUS said, just one way!"
   "I'll tell you, right now, I don't believe it!"   "Oh, I beg you to count the cost,
   JESUS said in the blessed HOLY BIBLE, without the shedding of Blood, all is lost!"

"I don't trust in your God or your BIBLE, and I'll bet my life there's no literal hell;
And a Blood sacrifice...that's repulsive; And there's no heaven in which to dwell.
   "I always say, eat, drink and be merry; A nice lady...a little fun...a glass of wine.
   I've worked hard and I surely deserve something; we only pass through life just one time."

"No drunkard shall enter the kingdom."   "But it's parties and pleasure that I crave."
"No reveler...nor fornicator...nor adulterer...these only lead to a sinner's grave."
   "I always live by my thought and my feelings, I don't care what the Good Book has to say;
   If there's a God, and a heaven, like you tell me...don't you worry, I'll make it some way!"

"You seem mighty proud of your doings, and your chest must stick out when you walk...
But get ready for a fall, my brother...You and the LORD need to have a little talk.
   For it's by grace, through faith, that we're forgiven, of ourselves we count all things but loss,
   And nothing else can bring us salvation...Nothing else...nothing short of the Cross!

The fear of the LORD is true wisdom, and the foolish heart does not believe,
But it's never too late to accept HIM; Just open your heart...and receive !
   Then some day we'll travel together, to that blessed, eternal, golden shore,
   When God gathers HIS children together, with HIM... eternally...forevermore!"

THE WAY

What must I do, you may ask me
To gain unending, everlasting life,
When I leave this world of pain and sin,
And turmoil, hate and strife?

Visit the sick if I have time,
Help a friend with a heavy load?
I'm proud of my life, my works and deeds,
I'm sure that I'm on the right road.

Lend a helping hand to a brother in need,
Do one good deed every day;
Pay all of my bills, give to charity?
I know this must be the right way.

Well, let me say you've accomplished a lot
As the world judges people today,
But let's take a look at the Word of God
And see what He Himself has to say.

It's not by works of righteousness we have done
But according to His mercy He saves;
By His Spiritual washing of regeneration
That we're set free from our sin that enslaves.

No, not by our toil, our works, our labor
Or anything else that we've done;
Not by our goodness, our riches, our virtue...
But by the shedding of blood by God's Son!

God is ready and willing to save you;
He is waiting for your confession of sin,
If you believe in your heart just call on His Name
So your Spiritual journey with Christ can begin!

THE WEAKEST LINK

I needed to raise my car for some repair
And I wondered what I would do.
So I got a chain hoist and began to pull
But a link in the chain pulled in-two.

This disappointing event caused me to think,
Only one of the links had broken,
Yet, one small link caused the chain to fail...
True words were never spoken.

Some would say that the weakest link
Was what caused the chain to fail,
And, if that is true there's another truth
I would like for someone to "unveil."

You see, there's another "chain...a sacred "chain,"
Where the very same principle must apply,
Where even the weakest link will cause the chain to fail...
Will someone please tell me why?

We have all heard of the Ten Commandments
That were given to govern our life,
And if we honor and cherish and obey them
There will be much more peace and less strife;

But which one is the most important?
That's a question we might long discuss,
So let's look at the list and consider,
For they all were given to us.

Shall we list them in order of importance?
That would be impossible for me;
We might get the first and the second...
But what will we list number three?

Is murder and killing, or adultery
Worse than stealing or cursing God's name?
What about honoring thy father and mother...
Is one greater, or all about the same?

And what about the least Commandment...
And, is our arrangement correctly done?
Remember, these Commandments are God's chain to us...
Ten links to the Almighty One!

What happens if just one link is broken,
One Commandment...be it great or small;
Just like the link in the chain, all our work is in vain...
Break ONE...and we're guilty of ALL!

James said it plain in chapter two, verse ten...
We are guilty of breaking God's Law.
We are all sinners, we are all condemned,
But that's what God in His wisdom foresaw,

And that's why Jesus came, why God sent His Son,
For by the law our sin nature is made known;
But God in His love and His mercy and grace
Was willing to sacrifice His very Own.

Yes, Jesus came to redeem us from the weakness of the law
To forgive us and pardon us of sin;
To free us, to save us, to cleanse us by His blood...
So new life within us can begin!

THE WILL

Just think for a moment the power of the "will"...
Have you ever stopped to realize,
You can take a step; you can raise your hand,
With the "will" you can close your eyes.

The highway we travel each day that we live
May be filled with good things or strife,
And this powerful "enigma" we call the "will"...
Will determine the course of our life.

Will you, or won't you, that's one of the questions
We all must face every day.
Sometimes it's easy; sometimes it's hard...
Sometimes we're not sure what to say.

You say yes, or no, you receive, you reject,
You may not realize it, but still...
You decide, you determine your pathway of life
By decisions you make with your "will."

You can choose right, you can choose wrong,
You are free to make your choice...
But sooner or later God will speak to you
In His tender, quiet, still, soft voice.

He's calling you to a higher choice,
"Come unto Me," says He.
Will you...or won't you...what do you say;
What will the answer be?

Before Jesus died He prayed, one day,
Perhaps from that very spot,
"Oh Jerusalem...Jerusalem...come unto Me!"
But they refused, they said No...they would not.

It's never too late as long as He calls.
It's never too late to choose.
You can say yes... you can still make that choice,
Or you can turn away and refuse.

The lame man asked to be fully healed;
And can't you imagine the thrill
When Jesus stopped and spoke the words,
"I will...I will...I will!"

The blind man asked to be given his sight,
Again Jesus said, "I will, I will."
He's now waiting for you...what do you say?
He's waiting...He's waiting, still?

THROUGH THE TEARS

Today I am so very sad,
Last night my mother left my dad,
But I can hardly blame her though,
He was a mixed up "so and so."

Oh, I really shouldn't talk like that,
But when he and mother had a spat
It always ended in a fight
And he would stay out late at night

Out with, who knows? And drinking, too,
And other things I know he'd do;
I will not tell just what they are
But I'll say this, "He went too far!"

I've heard them yell and hit and swear;
Oh how I wish I wasn't there,
And later on, one night I swore
I wouldn't stand it anymore.

"Listen, Dad...I must step in-between."
"Get out of here, you're just a teen!"
"I'm sorry, Dad...Is it my fault...
Don't you know this action has to halt!"

"Oh Dad, I want to love you, so,
But I can't, when you're like this, you know.
Can't we begin, anew, today...
I know there is a better way."

"There was a time when you weren't like this,
When Mother loved your tender kiss;
What things went wrong...What happened, Dad,
That's changed our lives, that's drove us mad?"

"It's hard to love you through my tears
Yet, when I think back to your tender years
And picture you as a wee, wee child...
Those big bright eyes, your loving smile;

So peaceful there in your little bed,
You were so sweet, Grandmother said,
A child so innocent, a life so new...
I can love you Daddy, and pray for you!"

When a person is on the witness stand he or she swears that they will tell the TRUTH, the WHOLE TRUTH, and nothing but THE TRUTH! But I don't think many people really know the Truth. This subject has to do with those who want to put the very name or mention of God or Jesus Christ out of our government, our government buildings, government land, government events, our schools and every walk of public society...and if this happens our Nation, and society, as we know it will CEASE to EXIST! But here is the odd thing about this subject, the very people who want to remove the very mention of God Or Jesus Christ are some of the biggest violators of what they protest. Let me explain...it has to do with **OUR DATING SYSTEM.** The following poem will explain it fully:

TIME WILL TELL ON YOU
???? ARE YOU REALLY HONEST????
???What Does 2015 Really mean ???

In 1492 Columbus came here, we know,
But what event in history made this date so?
"Whether it's 1776...or 2005,
What happened, years ago, that keeps this date alive?
   If we're measuring time and setting a date
   From what point in history do we calculate?
   "In 1492 Columbus came to our shore...
   But what happened 14 hundred and 92 years before?
All of our time, dates from this event..."
CHRIST CAME TO EARTH! GOD'S SON WAS SENT!
Take any paper, any book or magazine,
Look at the date, tell me, "What does each date mean?"
   Two thousand and fifteen, or so, years ago
   CHRIST came to earth because he loved us so;
   And everything in this world is a witness to
   CHRIST'S coming to earth to redeem me and you.
All clothing, all furniture, everything sold
Has a date of manufacture, whether new or old;
Every dollar you gamble, every coin you spend,
Bears a date that is a witness, of CHRIST, my friend!
   No matter what you say, no matter what you do,
   You depend on CHRIST...let me prove it to you.
   Even you who disbelieve, who mock and jeer,

169

Who deny your Maker...and act so cavalier;
You may think me crazy but before you celebrate...
Just remember this...all legal things must have a date.
Every title or certificate that is owned by you,
Whether car or home...every birth and marriage, too!
   You may have the right 'info' and file it away...
   But to stand up in court requires the year and the day!
   Every legal transaction, everything that is done,
   Points back to a date...the birth of GOD'S OWN SON.
And another question, please, just between you and me,
"What determines a date as BC. or AD.?"
You know LA or NYC or OKC...really mean a big City,
And if you don't know what BC or AD means...what a pity.
   These letters mean more than just letters, you see;
   What does July 4th... and 9-11 mean to you and me?
   It's been over 20 Centuries now since Christ Jesus came,
   God sent Him to earth by the power of HIS NAME;
It's the 21st Century now our records record,
2015 AD...Anno Domini...in the year of OUR LORD!
Every page in today's newspaper bears the dates 2015,
Please be honest and tell me exactly what they mean,
   There's over 700 witnesses of Christ in the car ads today,
   Tell me what does the year of each car you pass "say"?
   You can't run from CHRIST, and hide, that's true,
   You may think you are alone but HIS eye is watching you.
Some day my friend, when you lay in the cold, cold sod...
The date on your tombstone will declare the witness of God!
The "False Notion" of the separation of Church and State
Is what many misguided people spread and propagate;
   Nowhere in our Constitution are these words found...
   May God have mercy on those who spread it around!
   When writing or talking about a date, especially to our youth,
   Do you tell the real facts, do you tell the real truth?
Twenty one centuries have passed since CHRIST JESUS came,
"Do you believe in HIS WORK? Do you trust in HIS NAME?
There's absolutely no reason in this world, or out,
Why a scoffer should scoff...or a doubter should doubt;

170

Our dates bear the time of the witness, and seal,
And without this, my friend, you have no appeal.
365 days a year our calendars tell us when Jesus came,
Since God sent His to earth by the power of His name;
"So, what does 2015 really mean to you and me?"
CHRIST came, long ago, to set us free.
Whether you doubt...or deny...or reject HIS NAME...
Or believe and accept...the FACT remains the same!
Some want to change BC & AD to the "common Era" name
But the ABSOLUTE TRUTH will still be the same;
Any name or date used will still refer to this event,
When Jesus came to this earth, when God's Son was sent!
If we remove God, as many want, every mention of His Name
Our society, as we know it, will go up in ONE BIG FLAME!
All our records will be invalid, we cannot then use any date,
Our society will be destroyed...GOD have mercy on our fate!

TIME WILL TELL ON YOU!!!

If you agree with this please pass on to EVERYONE!!!!!!!!!!

TOO FAR

Do you think your life is so far from God
That He can't even hear your cry?
What a sobering thought, what fear that brings...
Where will you go when you die?
   The Bible tells us there is hope for us all
   Though our life is filled with sin,
   If we give our life to Jesus, He will forgive,
   That's when our new life in Him can begin.

Abraham served God but his nephew Lot
Moved to Sodom, that vile and wicked city.
But it cost him his home and everything,
And his wife turned to a pillar of salt... what a pity.
   His two daughters got him drunk and became pregnant
   By having sex with their own father, Lot.
   Their sons, Moab and Ammon, and descendants,
   Became Israel's enemies because of this sexual plot.

Years later, because of a famine, an Israelite family
Journeyed down to the Moabites land;
Their two sons found love and married a Moabitess,
And at first they thought that was grand.
   But Naomi's husband and two sons died
   And she decided to return to her home, and so...
   Her daughter-in-law Ruth resolved to follow her there,
   And said, "Wherever thou goest I will go."

After going to Israel, Ruth the Moabitess, married Boaz,
And they soon had a son named Obed;
Then Obed had a son named Jessie... and Jessie...
He had a son named David...enough said.
   These all, plus Rahab, were in the lineage of Jesus.
   Is your ancestry worse than the one above?
   Jesus will forgive and save the worst sinner,
   Because of His Grace, forgiveness and great LOVE!

Yes, there is hope for the vilest of sinners...
All we like sheep have gone astray,
All those who are saved, are sinners, saved by God's grace,
Will you accept Him as your Savior today?
    No one is too wicked or too far from the Savior...
    He is anxiously waiting to hear your cry.
    If you will not accept His forgiveness and salvation...
    Will you tell me why, Tell Me Why, TELL ME WHY?

TWO THIEVES

What about the two thieves who died with Jesus
On the cruel, and terrible, rugged cross?
One was saved by God's mercy and grace,
But the other thief suffered much more loss.

Not only did each loose his precious life,
But more important one lost his soul;
Their sinful lives probably dated back to youth
When they lived their lives out of control.

They both had lived their lives in vain,
Living a sinful life of shame and crime,
And for their chances of being forgiven
Most folks wouldn't have given a "dime."

One railed on the Lord as they hung on the cross,
He never sought the Lord nor repented of his sin,
But the other repented and called on the Lord,
Jesus said, "Today, with me, your new life will begin."

It's never too late to call on the Lord
When you're touched, and your heart is sincere;
When you repent and believe in God's saving grace
All the angels in Heaven rejoice, and give a cheer.

Have you come to Jesus in repentance of sin?
All we like sheep have gone astray;
No matter what you've done, no matter who you are,
If you'll call on Jesus He'll save you today.

WHAT DO YOU KNOW

What do you know, you know, you know;
Are all of your convictions really right and pure;
Does it matter at all what you actually believe,
And of how many things are you absolutely sure?

Well, that is a very sobering thought, at least to me
When I think of all the things there is to know;
If getting to heaven depends on me knowing everything
There's positively no chance I'll get to go.

But no one knows everything about our Lord
And many of His ways are past our finding out;
He said all of our wisdom is foolishness to Him,
But by faith we can know what His grace is about.

There are certainly things that we must believe;
One is, Jesus was crucified on the cross for our sins.
He was buried, and the third day He arose from the grave,
And that, my friend, is where our "knowing" begins.

He said we all have sinned and come short of His glory;
But if we confess He will forgive and give us eternal life.
He will give us peace, love, joy and assurance
Instead of unbelief, doubt, heartache and strife.

Our righteousness is as filthy rags to the Master;
If we could have earned it Jesus wouldn't have had to die,
But God loved us enough to sacrifice His only Son...
And outside of His "love" we will never understand why.

No, I will never know all of God's ways and His wisdom,
But there is one thing I KNOW...I'm happy to say,
I KNOW in Whom I have believed and am persuaded...
That He is able to keep my commitment against that "DAY"!

175

WHAT DOES IT MEAN?

Do you ever wonder when reading God's Word
How some things may seem hard to understand?
The Bible was written many hundred years ago
By many writers in a foreign language, and land.

It is often very hard to put thoughts into words
So the reader will know exactly what you say;
And many times the word meant something different
In the olden days than it does in our present day.

We ate breakfast, dinner and SUPPER when I grew up
But I see now folks have made a very big change;
They don't eat SUPPER, it's breakfast, lunch and dinner,
And to me that really seems mighty strange.

My lunch was something I carried in a sack or pail
And I ate it at 12 o'clock, dinner time, or noon,
But it was SUPPER we ate at the evening meal
And it could never, never come too soon.

I guess people can't take the Lord's Supper today
Because there's no such thing as SUPPER to them;
I suppose they could take a bite, and say a prayer
And close the Lord's DINNER with hymn.

Words and writings don't always mean what they say,
At least what they say, or seem to say to me,
So we must interpret many of the things we read,
And that's not always so pleasant and easy.

Are the 12 stones that Joshua set up in the midst of Jordan
Still standing there even unto this very day;
And when the Word says beyond, or on the other side of Jordan,
Which side of Jordan are you on, what does it say?

When we read that Jesus was the Lamb, or Shepherd,
Or the Bright and morning Star, or the Light,
To understand what the writer really meant to convey
There's something that we must do to get it right.

176

Certainly we must pray for the Spirit to guide us,
And sometimes it's hard to put an exact meaning into a word;
Paul tells us to compare spiritual things with spiritual,
And not believe every thing we might have heard.

When we read something...what does it say, what does it mean...
What does the reading really mean to me?
With prayer and study and leading of the Holy Spirit
I believe our "eyes" will be opened so we can "see."

WHAT IF! WHAT IF!

WHAT IF things haven't worked out exactly as you planned
And some things you "believed" aren't really true.
And though you tried hard in life to do what you thought best
This "old world" wasn't fair to you.

   You really don't know why things happened like they did;
    Why you haven't gained wealth or fame,
    And you've neglected your family and most of your friends...
    About all you have left is your name.

"Well, perhaps soon it will all be over
And I'll be FREE when I take my last breath.
I don't believe in this 'stuff' about a life hereafter,
NO...I don't believe in a life after death."

   But there's a puzzling question that you need to decide
    Before this life on earth is gone,
    WHAT IF...WHAT IF death doesn't end it all
    And our other life goes on and on?

WHAT IF life goes on in another world...
Just where could that world possibly be?
That's a most important question, perhaps the most,
Of all the things that face you and me!

   WHAT IF...WHAT IF the Bible is true
    And we don't just vanish away?
    Will you honestly, just now, ask yourself this question;
    Will you...will you do it, what do you say?

It seems a wise man would not possibly take that chance
But he would sincerely seek God's Truth,
Even though he had mocked and sneered and scoffed
All the days of his life from his youth.

WHAT IF...WHAT IF you happen to be wrong...
WHAT IF there is another life to live;
And WHAT IF you have waited too long to make a choice,
What would you be willing to give?

Would there be any profit if you gained the whole world
But in the end you lost your own soul?
You know, It would be too late to make a change
If you owned all the world and its gold!

What if there is a life after death;
There isn't a worthwhile thing you would've lost
But, if there is an afterlife in either heaven or hell...
Have you counted...have you counted the cost?

Jesus said, I am The Way, The Truth, The Life,
No one can come to the Father but by Me...
But the fool has said...there is NO GOD...
And there is absolutely NO ETERNITY!

WHAT MUST I DO

What must I do, you may ask me,
To earn this "Eternal Life"...
To escape this world of pain and sin
And turmoil, hate and strife?

I pay all of my bills, give to charity,
Do, at least, one good deed every day;
Lend a helping hand to a brother in need,
I know this must be the way.

And I visit the sick when I have time...
Or help a friend with his heavy load;
I'm proud of my life, my works and deeds,
I'm sure I'm on the right road.

Well let me say, you've accomplished a lot
As the world judges people today,
But let's take a look at the Word of God
And see what He has to say.

It's not by our works of righteousness that we do
But it's according to His mercy He saves,
By the "Spiritual Washing of Regeneration"
That we are set free from our sin that enslaves.

No, not by works, or toils, or accomplishments
Nor anything else we have done;
Not by our goodness, our riches, our virtue,
But by the shedding of blood by His Son.

Our good works do not count in God's plan of redemption,
We are sinners, condemned and lost;
Nothing we can do will clear or pay the debt,
That's why Jesus came and paid the cost.

He is ready and willing to save you,
To forgive any and all of your sins;
If you believe in your heart, just call on His name,
That's when a New Life in Jesus begins.

Now, our works do count if they are accomplished
In obedience to God's Holy Word and plan;
But salvation is a gift, by Grace, through Faith,
That's why Jesus gave his life for man.

WHO AM I?

Have you ever wondered about the "Mystery of Life"
And why you are who you are...
And not somebody else, or the opposite sex,
Or a monkey...or perhaps something more bizarre?

Some folks say, "I am just me,,,I'm only one,
And they will never make me another."
Well, part of that is true, we are certainly one,
But we are also "THREE," my brother!

One in three, three in one...Oh really;
Please tell me how that can be.
Well we are body, soul and spirit
And these three make a "Trinity."

Oft' times I may look in the mirror and think,
"I guess I am just what I see."
But this body is not exactly who I am
And what I see is not actually me.

I am a "Spirit" that inhabits a body
In this earthbound experience below;
Let me explain it a little more thoroughly
And see if you think it is so.

Like a space suit is required for travel in space,
Our bodies are much the same;
To survive as a human creature in this world of ours
Our "Spirit" must live in an earthly frame.

We are prone to judge lives like the books we see,
We take a glance at the cover and decide,
And miss the more important essence of life
Because we fail to look deeper inside.

We can loose an arm, we can loose a leg,
We might not even be close "to par"
And though we are limited in physical things,
We are still who we "truly are."

I know I'd be restricted if I lost these parts
In all of the things I'd be able to do,
But I'm a "Spirit"...my mind, will, and emotions
Are literally Me...a "Living Soul"...that is true!

Yes, my mind, my will and my emotions, I believe,
Set my "Soul" apart, you see,
From everyone and everything in this vast universe
And are the things that make ME really "ME."

But as long as my "Spirit" resides here on this earth
I am an earthbound, living "Soul,"
Subject to the boundaries and limits set forth
By the "One" who is in control.

And this house of clay that we live in today
Is surely not all of who we are;
We didn't choose it, some day we'll lose it,
But we'll still be who we really are.

Yet we are stewards and keepers of our humble abode
Though it's a temporary dwelling place,
For it's absolutely essential to remain on this globe
As long as we occupy time and space.

Yes, to exist as a living soul on this earth
We, a "Spirit," must have a place to dwell;
And without a human "Spirit" living within
Our body is just an empty shell.

Truly, our sojourn here is an incredible thing
And I wonder just how many understand,
That when we leave the confines of this earth behind
We will journey to another land.

Our existence in time will surely come to an end,
Our day of departure may be nigh,
Then, this house will crumble and decay away...
But we ourselves, our "Spirit," will not die.

FAMILY

A GO-GETTER

Some folks like traveling and some folks like hiking
And some folks like riding a bike;
Some folks like movies, and watching TV,
And some folks don't know what they like.

Some folks just grumble and struggle through life
And don't know one end from the other.
I know one or two, on my life's journey here,
And they're a pain to be around...Oh Brother!

But I know a guy who is opposite to this;
He knows exactly where he stands
And he has made a very respectable life,
And he has done it with his mind and his hands,

He owns his own company and has a new home,
A new truck, a car...and a cat;
A barn, a tractor, a garden, a lake;
He's a get-up-and-goer...how's that?

He likes golfing and racing and hunting and fishing
And a close and exciting ball game;
And he has a partner who is a reflection of him...
Hey, their likes are almost exactly the same.

And he married a beautiful "queen of a gal."
I think I'll shout his praises real LOUD;
And, you know what...he's my son-in law,
Brad Alan Roberts...I'm Real PROUD!

A HOUSE OR A HOME

Almost everyone's dream is to build or own a new home,
That seems to be a part of the marriage dream,
But many work and labor years and years
But don't achieve, because it's harder than it may seem.

We can't see tomorrow and we don't always know why
We weren't able to reach our lifetime goal,
But there's something more important than building a house,
What about the importance of our Eternal Soul?

As I drove down the road and saw the beautiful houses
A sober and chilling thought raced through my mind,
If we knew the relation of the children, husband and wife,
I wonder what in the world we would find?

There's so much worldliness in living relations today,
Many don't marry and many don't really love their mate,
Many houses have 4 stall garages and are 3 stories high,
But a house is not a HOME if it's filled with sin and hate!

Many houses are not HOMES, there's little or no love.
They're full of turmoil, heartache and pain;
You may build a big house, but that doesn't make it a HOME,
Unless the Lord builds the house your labor is all in VAIN!

A SPECIAL SOMEONE
My oldest granddaughter

I know a precious little girl,
Her name is Stephanie,
She lives so very far away,
Away across the sea.

She crossed the wide, wide ocean
And her grandma got to hold,
Her first granddaughter in her arms
When she was two weeks old.

She'd rock her in her rocking chair
And she would always keep
Her tiny head against her cheek
Until she'd fall asleep.

What a thrill to keep this bundle
Snuggled close against her breast,
Just to feel her faintest heartbeat
And to know she was at rest.

Now I would like to pick her up
And squeeze her, oh so tight,
And hug her neck, and kiss her,
And tuck her in at night.

I know that she is very sweet
And getting mighty pretty,
And soon I'll get to see her
In my home in Midwest City!

A SPICE OF GINGER

My middle daughter

There are certain kinds of spices
That grow across the sea,
Some use them in their cookies,
Some use them in their tea.

They call the spices GINGER,
"We love the taste," they say.
It's put in many, many things;
People use it every way.

Some folks use GINGER spices
To make GINGER-cakes and ale;
My mother made me GINGER-snaps
Each Sunday, without fail.

Some mothers really like to make
A man of GINGER-bread,
Or many little GINGER-boys
With frosting on their head.

There's a special kind of GINGER
That is sweeter yet, to me,
I used to hold and handle her
So GINGER-ly...my GINGER LEE!

Yes, she's my precious daughter,
Ever loving...ever true,
I'm so proud and happy
To have a "GINGER-girl" like you!

Now, GINGER has a "GINGER-man"
Who is really mighty fine,
Together they're a lovely pair...
The best you'll ever find!

Aunt Opal's Funnies

Little Robin Red Breast jumped upon the wall, Pussy Cat jumped up after him and almost had a fall. The little Robin chirped and sang and what did Pussy say? Pussy Cat said "Meow" "Meow" and Robin flew away.

A woodpecker pecked on a Church House door. He pecked and he pecked 'till his pecker got sore.

Kercheek, Kercheek, cabickery ben, come out of the woods and we'll sand-paper your chin. We're wild, we're wooly, we're notched like a saw, Scotland, Scotland, RAH, RAH, RAH!!!

My Daddy was all dressed up today. He never looked so fine. I thought when I first looked at him, my Daddy wasn't mine. He's got a dandy fine new suit, the old one was so old. It's brown he wears, it's Eagle too, I guess it must be gold. So my Daddy just belongs to my dear Mother, and I guess the folks are blind that cannot see. For his buttons are marked U.S. and that spells us I guess. So he just belongs to Mother Dear and me.

What king of wood, would a woodpecker peck, if a woodpecker would peck wood, he'd peck: hardwood, softwood, redwood, dogwood, cottonwood, ply-wood, hickory and beech, rosewood, teakwood, sandlewood and candlewood walnut, hazel nut, apple and peach; in oak trees, elm trees, fur trees, pear trees, pine trees, shoe trees and telephone poles, barn doors, benches, table tops and fences. A woodpecker would peck a peck of little holes.

BIG TROUBLE
by Bill "Grandpa" Swain

Itty, bitty, Ryan Swain,
Sweet as sugar cane,
No, no, must disdain,
Him one big pain!

All night has lain,
Bawl, bawl, complain, complain,
Sleep, sleep, can't attain,
Him one "rattle brain."

Me open window pane,
Stare out across terrain,
Big trouble very plain,
Him tinkle like rain.

Carpet wet, carpet stain,
Wee wee must contain,
Heart throb, big migraine,
Dry diaper can't obtain,

Him scream, scream, strain,
Fight like hurricane,
Me try to constrain,
Wife cry, me abstain.

Next, try to entertain,
Peace, quiet to regain,
Blood rush through vein,
Me try once again.

Small hope now wane,
Him raise more Cain,
Him act inhumane,
All hope in vain,

Little fellow can't explain
But him drive Dad insane!
Tie up with chain,
Wrap on minnow seine,

Beat with walking cane,
Hang on weather vane.
Our trouble still remain,
Maybe flush him down drain,

Get bottle of champagne,
Might even try cocaine.
Jump on airplane,
Run away to Spain...

Me STOP,,,must refrain,
My composure can't retain,
Big laugh, can't restrain,
Me joke, my chicane,

Little William Ryan Swain
Sweeter than sugar cane,
My love still remain,
Him Our BIG GAIN!

BILLS BILLS BILLS
My Son

A lot of people get real sick
When all their BILLS arrive,
   Then the sick must see a doctor
   And make more BILLS to keep alive.
The doctor puts them in the bed
Prescribing pills to cure their ills,
   But the only way to stop their pain
   Is with stacks of dollar BILLS!
Each month the BILLS grow higher
For their cars and homes and clothes,
   All through their lives...and after,
   They'll be paying through their nose!
There's not much hope to look ahead,
It almost blows one's mind...
   Even all the birds and ducks have BILLS
   But at least they're not "behind!"
Now, I didn't always feel this way,
About the BILLS, I mean,
   I did hate some...but some I like,
   And some were in-between.
But there is one special BILL I love
That's been growing day by day;
   I used to take him in my arms
   And we would laugh and play.
He's come a long, long way since then,
Since he was my baby boy,
   Today he is a grown-up man
   And he fills my heart with joy!

COMING OF AGE
A Word for Young Folks and Old Folks

This girl was a super attraction,
I mean the kind that will spin your head;
She was all dressed out in her fancy jeans
And a flashing blouse of red.

   Her appearance and smile were so charming,
   Her figure and height were just right,
   Her lips and her looks…so alluring,
   Her manner and walk...a delight.

She gave more than a glance as she passed me,
My temperature started to rise,
The most beautiful thing that these eyes had seen
Was now passing before my eyes!

   And before I knew what was happening
   My emotions were filled with... with desire.
   My intentions were facing a testing
   And I needed help to put out the fire.

Something strange had affected my thinking,
Weird sensations... and the craziest "dreams"...
Well, sometimes they're rational and noble
But mostly they run to extremes.

   I don't rightly know how all these feelings
   Can drive a sane fellow into a rage,
   And change a teen's outlook on women...
   Guess my hormones are coming of age!

It took time to regain my composer
And clear the cobwebs from my head,
Meanwhile, some scripture had come to mind
And I thought about what it said.

One has no greater treasure than VIRTUE,
So don't let anyone take it away,
And don't be anxious to give it so freely,
For, once gone, it's gone FOREVER...to stay!

Predetermine your boundaries and limits,
Count the cost before it's too late,
And think how you'd want your sister
To be treated while out on a date.

I remember when girls held no interest,
And they must have felt mutually the same,
Now we both search for...love and fulfillment...
And we both, sometimes, cheat at the game.

But how will I face my tomorrows
If I plunder and rob and steal,
Or...if I take what is sometimes given...
A treasure so precious and real.

I must pledge as I face these temptations
No "if you love me you'll let me" from me,
And, like JOB, in his hour of temptation,
Make a covenant with his eyes not to "see."

I have a treasure I want to keep HOLY
Until the right time comes my way,
For all things have a right season...
And, the right "season" is not today!

COUNTRY LIVING

It's an inhumane form of voluntary captivity!
>That's the way that I felt when I lived in the city.
Then a great thing happened that changed my life...
>I moved to the country with my kids and wife.

In the evenings you can hear the whippoorwills cry
>And the crickets will chirp their own lullaby;
The bullfrogs will croak and the locusts sing
>And the rabbits hop by without thinking a thing.

On many a night you can hear coyotes bark,
>And the raccoons come out at night in the dark;
The birds and squirrels sing and play in the trees,
>And the leaves sing a sweet melody in the breeze.

The kids "whoop it up" ever now and then,
>With a neighbor...or with a new friend
And the "whoot" owl may "whoot" at three...or four...
>It's a far different life than what I knew before.

But all of these new sounds that I now hear
>Are such sweet, sweet music to my ear;
No more honking horns...no more racing cars...
>No squeaking brakes...no squealing tires!

Oh, it's great out here with my family,
>Where the water is pure and the air is free;
If you have had bad memories that you want to erase...
>Just get yourself a "quiet" country place!

DEAREST DARLING

You are such a sweet, sweet sweetheart,
  Always pleasant, always kind,
Friends and family know that you're
  As sweet as sweet as anyone can find!

When you were just a wee, wee babe
  Your Mom and Daddy used to hold
Their blessed gift from heaven
  And watch your little life unfold.

They'd rock you in the rocking chair
  And they would always keep
You tiny head against their cheek
  Until you'd fall asleep.

What a thrill to have their baby
  Snuggled close against their breast,
Just to feel your faintest heartbeat
  And to know you were at rest.

All the days you've been together
  They have always shared your love,
Through the joys and through the sorrows
  With God's help from up above.

Like the lovely flowers of springtime
  And the beauty of the land,
Your fragile, tender days of childhood
  Shows the touch of God's own hand.

Yes, you're a very precious person,
  As pure as heaven's morning dew,
Your parents are so very blessed
  To have a priceless child like you!

God knew they had a longing,
  Something missing, something wrong,
And then He gave you to them...
  At God's right time you came along!

196

DIXIE

In this world there's lots of DIXIES,
I will mention some to you,
DIXIE music, DIXIE jazzes,
DIXIE plates and cupcakes, too.

DIXIE-dogs, and cafeterias,
DIXIE hats that someone sells,
Deep down in the "Heart of DIXIE"
There are lovely DIXIE Bells.

And I know there's DIXIE Darlings,
Let me name just three or four;
Ginger Lee and Terri Lynn,
William Ralph...and there's one more.

I remember nineteen-fifty,
In January of that year,
The Twenty-seventh, something happened,
I made you mine, that night, my Dear!

And, ever since we've been together,
Sixty-one years we've shared our love,
Through the joys and through the sorrows,
With God's help from up above.

I want to praise and thank You, Darling,
For all you've done, and mean to me;
Our precious love will live forever...
Through All Time and ETERNITY!

FATHER

Although my father died when I was 5 months,
This is who I think my Father would have been.

I am so proud to look up to a man like you,
Whose every way and walk is strong and true;
    Your life is a witness that all can see,
    A most precious gift from God to me.

How I cherish each moment we have lived and shared,
Just to feel and to know how much you have cared,
    You toil, unceasingly, throughout the day
    Yet, somehow, find time for a little play.

You work so hard for our daily bread
Without concern for yourself or what others said,
    But it's not just the things you so freely give,
    For much more to me is the life that you live.

When I am discouraged and can't see my way
You always take time to encourage and pray.
    You have proved your unfailing love for me...
    Above everything else...that is the key!

I'm so thankful to tell of your unmeasurable love,
It's so much like our Savior's in Heaven above,
    For long after the days you have lived, and gone...
    My father's great love will still live on!

GROWING OLDER

There's two ways of looking at everything
    In this world, as we're passing through,
The "High Way" and the "Low Way"
    How you see it is up to you.

One says, "I'm growing old and feeble,
    All of my old friends are gone,
I really don't have anyone left,
    I feel so all alone.

"Why has all of my family departed
    And I'm left to linger alone?
No one cares or comes to see me,
    They won't miss me when I'm gone.

"The world looks so dark and hopeless,
    It's different in so many ways,
And nothing looks good about it
    Like it did in the good old days.

"I've discovered one thing growing older,
    Life just keeps getting worse;
Just surviving is not really living...
    Existing like this is a curse."

Another says, "I'm growing old and feeble.
    All of my old friends are gone
But I have made so many new ones
    I never feel all alone."

All of my family has gone on before me
    But I thank God for the length of my life,
His word daily comforts and cheers me
    As it did my dear, precious wife.

"The world looks so dark and hopeless,
    It's different in so many ways,
But there's victory for me in Jesus
    And to every one who prays.

"I've discovered new things, growing older,
    Some exciting, I'm happy to say,
And when it comes time to leave it behind
God will go with me...All the way!"

HOW INDIANS GOT THEIR NAME

Gather 'round all you folks, take a seat at the table,
I'll tell you some stories, I think I am able,
About some long ago times and some different faces,
About some little known people and some little known places.

About how they got their names and where they use to play,
And many more things done in an unusual way;
How some children played , and some went to school...
And most everything was governed by a different rule.

Okay...Okay, Yes I heard you yellin'
That you're ready to listen to my story tellin'.
I'll do my utmost best, since you're takin' the time,
So listen real closely to these words of rhyme.

We were part of the Oil Boom...and we had much celebration
Helping our new State become a part of the Nation.
There were no on-line computers, no cell phones nor TV,
But we were mighty blessed...we were a part of HISTORY!

Some people called us OKIES...but we really didn't mind,
We just gave 'um a smile and tried to be kind.
We're talking about OKLAHOMA..."Land Of The Red Man".
I'll give some Indian names...and how our story began.

Most Indian names may seem kind-of strange to you,
Like Tiger, Snake and Wildcat, and Crazyhorse, too.
But what about the "whiteman's" names, of Smith, Baker and Cook?
They were named for what they did, just you take a look,

And so with many "red man"...after some happening or event,
He was known by that name forever, wherever he lived or went.
I think it's kind-of easy to see how "Straight-Arrow" got his name
For with his bow and arrow he won honors and great fame.

He could always hit his target, from very far or near,
He killed many and many a turkey and also many deer.
A really, really great archer is much like "Superman"
He has always been very valuable ever since time began.

And from a rugged forest trail where a wounded trapper laid,
He was found, rescued and nursed to health by a lovely Indian Maid.
It was in her father's teepee near the raging river Big Horn;
They fell in love, were married...and soon a son was born.

He was a happy little fellow, always smiling, never sad,
They named the baby "White Chief" in honor of his dad.
He grew up to be a hunter, killing buffalo and deer,
He had great strength and nerves of steel, never showing pain nor fear.

And "Lone Wolf" was another lad whose name may seem so strange,
He wandered about just by himself all over the open range.
He'd usually stay away all day and sometimes part of the night
But he was always up in the morning before the sun shone bright.

So just like the lone, gray wolf who never stayed with the pack,
You were never sure of where he'd been when you saw him coming back.
The pack was seldom around the lone wolf, they never tarried nor stayed,
They soon traveled on in their usual pack because he never played.

But there was one Real "old gray wolf" who was now well past his prime,
They found out later that's where this lad was spending most of his time,
Making friends with the "enemy...the old gray wolf"...most everybody said;
Something's wrong with this Indian lad, he's sure not right in the head.

They call him "Gray wolf" and tease him a lot, but he became a great man.
When he was grown he became "Chief Gray Wolf" and ruled over all the land.
Sometimes there's greatness in people that no one ever sees
Until that one is put to the test...and they pass that test with ease.

There's a place I often visit called the Wildcat Hollow Cave.
I've heard this story often, about an Indian lad so brave.
It's a lovely place to visit now but it wasn't always so;
It was a home for wildcats, at a time not long ago.

The lad had crawled into the cave not knowing what lay ahead,
For if he knew he surely would have made another choice instead.
The mother wildcat was not all that pleased for someone to invade her lair
So, with lightening speed, and snarled fangs, with claws and bristled hair

She sprang upon the startled lad and he had no time to think,
He had no time for anything...not even time to blink...
Except...He had to fight like a "wildcat" if he was to survive;
He doesn't know how but he fought her off, and today he is alive.

He must have fought like a "wildcat"...like his name now applies,
That's how Mr. "Wildcat" got his name...and he still has both his eyes.
So you see it's not so unusual how each Indian got his name,
Many other people in years gone by got their name exactly the same.

And "Black Bear" was another name of a strong, brave Indian boy.
He didn't have much but guess what he got for his very first "little boy" toy?
It wasn't a car, it wasn't a ball, a TV or radio,
It was a very special Indian gift...an arrow and a bow.

And little "Black Bear" grew stronger, with every passing day,
He helped his mother and his dad and still had time for play.
But what he liked best was to shoot an arrow at a target, or anything,
He became so skilled he could shoot a rabbit, or a turkey "on the wing."

One day when he and "Eagle Eye" were out playing on the hill
They heard a noise that scared the boys and gave them both a chill!
It wasn't an eagle, a hawk, a snake, or the roaring of a lion
That made them shake and turn around and look back far behind.

"It is a bear," said Eagle Eyes, "He went behind a tree.
He thinks he'll hide from both of us but he can't hide from me"
Yes, "Eagle Eyes" was the very best if there was anything around,
He could spot a bird or wolf or snake or a rabbit on the ground.

201

He could look across the plains and spot a deer or buffalo,
It may be kind of hard to believe, but it was really so.
I guess the lads were afraid to run so they remained real quiet,
But it wasn't long before the bear came directly in their sight.

"Black Bear" made ready his bow and arrow, and remained very still,
But the hungry bear kept coming, he was now on top of the hill.
Suddenly he turned his head and headed the scared boys way.
What happened next turned out for the best...I'm very happy to say!

The arrow traveled straight and true...and the bear fell to the ground.
The happy lads gave a BIG "war whoop" and danced around and around.
A black bear rug still rests upon "Black Bear's" teepee floor;
I could tell other tales about "Black Bear" if I had time for more.

Now, how do you think some got their names...I'll bet you really can;
"Tall chief"?...Yes, that's right, he was the tallest man.
And "Big Chief"?...Yes, he was big, and muscled and strong,
And when he was around you did obey...you didn't do anything wrong.

And I'll bet you can guess about the one they called "Little Blue Eyes."
Her eyes had much more sparkle than the stars up in the skies.
Oh my!...What a bundle of joy...and what a woman she became,
All of the tribes, everywhere around, knew of her beauty and fame.

And "Running Deer"...Oh Wow! He was one fast Indian brave.
He has the speed and endurance that all Indian warriors crave.
He can run all day or night, through the forests, hills or plains;
He never stops or slows nor rests, and he never, never complains.

When the big, fat, fleecy, white clouds came and floated across the sky,
This one little Indian Brave would stop, and watch and wonder why.
In the clouds he'd see "people" and "animals and things he'd never seen;
To him it was a fantastic show, just like on our movie screen.

The marvelous, magic things he saw fascinated the Indian child;
As he watched the Heavenly Artist's work his thoughts ran fast and wild.
The clouds fanned his imagination, that's how "Chief White Cloud" got his name;
So, next time the fluffy, white clouds appear, take a look, and do the same.

And the story about "Six Shooter"...that's quite a name for an Indian, I'd say.
They tell me all of this happened while he was out hunting, one day.
It was early one cold morning, the ground was covered with frost,
He found a six-shooter pistol that some reckless cowboy had lost.

He had seen and heard some cowboy out riding and shooting his gun,
And it looked to this Indian Brave like he was having a barrel of fun.
This six-shooter was his prize possession; it was always by his side;
Old "Six Shooter" kept it and treasured it until the day he died.

"Black Hawk" and "Goose" were two Indian boys who were very, very good friends.
They lived near the foot of the mountain where the beautiful river bends;
Where the fishing was always exciting and the hunting was always great,
And they always thanked the "Big Spirit" for every meal they ate.

While out running and playing, near the fast flowing river, one day
They each found a bird that was wounded, or so the folks all say.
Perhaps they were wounded by someone, or a fox or wolf or bear,
These kindhearted boys rescued the birds and gave them tender care.

The goose and the black hawk became their pets and their good "friends"
That's how these laddies got their names...and how this story ends.
There are many more Indian names like "Crazyhorse, Longknife and Snake"
And if I told you all of the others I don't think you'd stay awake.

But there is one more great Indian story I really would like to tell,
It's about a little Indian boy whose body was not so well.
At first he couldn't walk or run and he sure couldn't jump very high;
And at a very early age they didn't know if he would live or die.

But in time he overcame these odds and he grew to be very strong,
And he became a great warrior and chief, and his life span was very long;
But his early illness left its mark, and his legs were bowed, you see;
Yes, this Billy was bowlegged, as bowlegged as could be.

But that early illness didn't keep him from becoming an Indian Chief,
And some of his bravery and exploits goes almost beyond belief.
In Florida, the American Government tried to defeat this Indian man
But the brave "Chief Billy Bowlegs" now had another plan.

His life, a legend, and the wars he fought make quite an interesting story;
The U.S. agreed and "Billy Bowlegs" led the Seminoles to the Indian Territory.
And the little Oklahoma town where I grew up, and where I attended school,
Where I played and studied and was married, and learned the Golden Rule

That town became quite famous due to those untamed Oil Boom days.
I hope you can see if you never give up, the outcome always pays;
For the little town of BOWLEGS, was so named for a once, crippled man,
My friend, If you can "Top" this story...Then "Top" it if you can!

I WONDER

Some kids just don't have a Mom like I have,
Or a Dad on whom they depend,
They really don't have a family at all
Or a decent, dependable friend.

This life must seem cruel, this world so cold,
When you're facing it all alone,
When you're reaping the harvest of other's mistakes
And not just from seeds that you've sown.

Sometimes I forget how tough that it is
When there's no one to stand by your side,
No one to share all your burdens and pain...
And nowhere to go and hide.

I've never been shifted from house to house,
From family to family, not my own,
And been forced to face such trials of life,
And walk every step alone.

Oh, I'm thankful, Dear Lord, for my family and friends,
And all the good things you've given me,
If I had to live the life that some live,
I wonder just where I would be?

INDIAN TERRITORY

In the old Indian TERRItory
There are some TERRIfic things,
Big, big wide open spaces
And all that summer brings.

There's many happy kids at play
Doing things they love to do,
Some lucky ones own TERRIers
And calves and horses, too.

And there is one TERRIfing thing,
When tornados cross the sky,
But few other things are TERRIble,
I'll tell you the reason why.

Many, many years ago
Our family was quite small,
Just Dixie Lee and William O.
And no one else...that's all.

But a tiny bundle came along
That we never thought could be,
TERRI changed our life, completely,
And made us happy...TERRIbly!

This cute and active little girl
Was worth her weight in gold,
When God finished her He smiled a bit
And threw away the mold.

Now, she has traveled far and wide,
And among her collections, they say,
Are a handsome husband and two kids,
And another on the way.

JUST IN TIME
My oldest grandson

I have a little grandson
But he moved so far away,
I hope that he will come back soon
So we can laugh and play.

I know he goes to school each day
With other girls and boys;
He's learned to read and write his name
And pick up all his toys.

He's a handsome little fellow
That everyone should meet;
He's always kind, and smiling,
And his manner always sweet.

But he is growing up so fast...
I hope he don't forget
His Grandma and his Pappa
When he gets off the jet.

I didn't have a grandson
For so many, many years,
And, Oh, it made me lonely,
Sometimes I'd shed some tears.

God knew I had a longing,
Something missing, something wrong,
And then He gave me JUSTIN...
JUST-IN time he came along!

MEMORIES OF A BROKEN HOME

Thank the Lord, I have never had this problem but I offer my sympathy to those who have!

Suddenly, as if a shade
  Was drawn across the sky,
Thick clouds of doubt swept over me,
  My hopes began to die.

My world began to darken
  As my hate shut out the light;
My dreams and aspirations died
  In the blackness of that night.

This perfect marriage plan of God
  Lay stained and scarred by man...
How can the evil of this world
  Fit in the Master's plan?

My mind it cannot fathom,
  So I ask Thee, Lord, "Pray tell"
How a little bit of "Heaven"
  Turned into a living "Hell?"

And even now as I recall
  Those days of yesteryears,
I have to pause...and close my eyes,
  And wipe away the tears.

MOTHER

My father was buried on my mother's 18th birthday. She was a widow for 62 years.

How can we tell of Mother's love?
It reaches to the heavens above,
And on the earth where children trod
Her touch is like the touch of God.

She rises early, labors long,
Surrounds each sorrow with a song,
Faces all her problems with a prayer,
Bathes every task with loving care.

Her voice is like the morning dove,
Her words are filled with tones of love,
Her hopes are high, her faith is strong...
Returns a Right for every Wrong.

Her days are weary, vacations few,
But every thought always of you;
My work is spread from sun to sun...
But Mother's work is never done.

All that I do, all that I am,
Whether great or small, obscure, renown,
All that I ever hope to be,
I owe it...Mother...all to thee!

MY EPITAPH

When I come to the end of my journey
  And look back at my walk and my way,
Here are some of the things I hope I did
  And the things I hope you can say:

You made my hopes a little brighter,
  The raging storms a little quieter,
My lonely days a little fewer,
  The darkening skies a little bluer:

My heavy load a little lighter,
  Our friendship bonds a little tighter,
My aim in life a little truer,
  My words and thoughts a little purer;

You brought to me a little laughter,
  Cheer for my hurt, right then...and after,
I knew on you I could depend...
  Unto the end...you were my Friend!

SIX OF ONE

Your Mom and Dad are really, real glad
To know you're one fine son,
And Grandma and Grandpa can't find one flaw
In our latest grandson...JONATHAN!

Our family has been through its ups and downs
But "Someone" is making amends;
When grandchildren like you keep coming along
Our pride and joy never ends.

We've been many places and saw many faces
And observed grandkids, far and wide,
But the best we have found in the whole, wide world
Are the ones that we have by our side!

You're the sixth to arrive and, hey, man alive...
I don't know how many more there'll be,
But if they keep getting better and better each time
We may "SHOOT" for another two or three.

They're cheaper by the dozen, a lot of folks say,
But, per chance, if some folks have their "druthers"
We'll stick with the six that we already have
And not try for that "half-dozen others!"

The more the merrier has been our philosophy
But the Miller kids now number, FOUR,
And if the story they tell us is only half-true...
There AIN'T gonna be any MORE!!!!

SWEET HEARTS

Sweet things usually come in small packages,
If it's true what most folks say,
Like those heart shaped boxes of goodies
Made especially for Valentine's Day.

And many sweet hearts are made from chocolate
With nuts or candy or cherries inside,
And you never know on that special day
What the covering is trying to hide.

Some folks like hearthstone mints or cookies,
Even an ice cream cake, some say;
But what is the very best kind of sweet heart
That one can have on Valentine's Day?

Well, the kind of sweet heart that I like best
Is not made of candy or cake;
It won't make you sick if you get too much,
And maybe give you the tummy-ache.

You don't find it at the shops or stores
Where all the candy hearts will be;
No, it's a sweet heart of a different kind
That means the most to me.

But I much prefer this other SWEETHEART,
Yes, more than my words can tell,
'Cause she's my newest granddaughter,
Little Miss KELLI MICHELLE!

THE CINCINNATI KID

Some folks may call us children
And some folks call us kids;
Some kids make it to the top
And some kids hit the skids.

It's hard to tell when you look ahead
Where some "ornery" kid might land;
He might land up in the county jail...
Or be President of our land.

He might gain millions, or be destitute,
Or climb to the ultimate heights;
He might be kind, or be a prude
And always demand his rights.

We just don't know what the future holds,
When some kid steps out on his own,
And we may be surprised how well they turn out
After some of these kids are grown!

Now the Cincinnati Kid, he turned out well;
He served his country and God and man,
And he's dedicated himself to all of these,
And he'll do even more if he can.

The Kid married my daughter, now they have four kids
Who will soon be going their own way,
And all of "this" because of the CINCINNATI KID...
Who's my son-in-law...I'm proud to say!

THE FAMILY ALBUM

Of all the treasures in this world
I've surely had my due,
They're all around me, everywhere,
Perhaps you have some. too.

I'm really rich, I own a lot...
If, by chance, you didn't know
I'll try to show a few to you
And, perhaps you'll say it's so.

Here's some faded pictures from the past
All worn and stained with tears...
In my picture album of "memories"
That stretches across the years.

Here's a picture of my precious wife
Sitting quietly in her chair,
And a darling angel by her side
With locks of golden hair.

And see this priceless, little girl,
I once held her on my knee...
She's my very youngest daughter
And she's as sweet as sweet can be!

These are some longtime friends of mine,
And these pictures of this lad;
I'm mighty proud to say that I'm
Still claiming to be his dad.

And these over here are my pride and joy,
I keep them aside from the rest;
And I always save the best 'till the last
'Cause my grand kids are the best!

This boy came first, and then this girl,
And this girl was the last to arrive...
That is, until this fellow came...
And, "Oh my"...what a guy... "MAN ALIVE!"

He's the latest grandchild in the family
And was born in July, just passed,
He's the last in our shower of blessings
But I don't know how long that will last.

Yes, summer has come...and ended,
And winter will come with its snow,
But I feel all warm and peaceful inside
And my heart feels all aglow.

THE KILLER DILLER

Name me some occupations
That are honorable and good:
A doctor or a lawyer
Or a fashioner of wood.

A cowboy or a farmer,
Secretary or a teacher,
Policeman or a postman,
A surveyor or a preacher.

A mechanic or a housewife,
A merchant or a miller...
A Miller...well I know one
But she's a "killer diller!"

She's really not the kind of girl
I'd want to be my wife,
But I love to pitch some "woo" with her,
She spices up my life.

And when I say sweet things to her
She rolls those great big eyes...
And when it comes to giving LOVE
This gal will take the prize!

But she's really not a naughty girl
Like some "babes" I've heard say,
She's my sweet, Sweet, SWEET granddaughter,
And her name...Alanna Shea!

THE LAND OF IN-BETWEEN

While we were out for a walk my friend and I
Saw these good looking boys last week,
They looked our way and gave us the "eye"...
Guess they both were too bashful to speak.

It was a little unusual for such handsome guys
Not to whistle...or say even a word,
So I said to my friend, "Some cool, cool men;"
What a surprise when the two overheard.

They blushed a bit and we walked on ahead
But all the time they were still on our mind,
And we hadn't gone far when we realized
They were following a few steps behind.

We giggled, at first, and exchanged some choice words
As the excitement started to rise;
Would this lead the way to a perfect day
Or,,,were we in for a big surprise?

We soon learned of the fellow's intention,
Their aspirations and plans for us two;
Our family photos were not their main interest,
And you can bet it was not our I.Q.

Deep inside my emotions were racing,
My heart fluttered like leaves in the breeze,
Something told me I had better be careful...
But somehow I wanted to please.

These new feelings are all so confusing
When we reach the age of a teen;
No longer a child...but not yet grown up...
We are in "The Land of IN-BETWEEN!"

We don't understand these...these sensations we feel
And these new feelings we...we want to pursue;
Should we...or shouldn't we...we're all mixed up,
Someone help us, please...what must we do?

My Dear, don't yield to these fleshly temptations,
Seek the answer from the Lord up above,
He will give you strength, deliverance and direction,
Just trust His Word and rest in His LOVE!

THE NAME'S THE SAME

There are so many guys around,
There are some so big and tall,
And some so "teeny-weeny"
They are hardly guys at all.

But irregardless of your size
Or what ever you happen to do,
One of the most important things to me
Is the name that was given to you.

I thought a bit about my name
When I was just a kid,
But things have changed and now I think
More than I ever did.

At first I thought that my own name
Would not be carried on,
It's not worth much, I used to think...
And then I had a son.

That changed my thinking quite a bit
And now I want to say,
The day that William Ralph was born
Was a mighty happy day.

I guess William Ralph and William O.
And William T. were not enough...
' Cause now William Ralph...has a William Ryan
And we think William Ryan is "hot stuff!"

Not because his name is William,
Too many Williams can be a pain,
So we'll just call him Ryan...
But he still is another Swain.

Do you ever think about a name
And what a name may mean,
Whether it's important...or a joke,
Or somewhere in-between?

The name "Swain, they say, means "a lover"
And I can tell you, it surely is true,
Because now I have a new grandson...
And, Mr. Swain, I sure do love you!

THIS NEW LIFE   This one is for us old folks

We know time changes everything, that's one thing I'll admit,
But life doesn't seem that different...it's just the way we look at it.
   You kids say there's a few things, though, we need to rearrange,
   'Cause I'm in my second childhood,...so I guess there'll be a change.

You tell me when you talk to me, the time has finally come;
But life isn't all that different, it's just the side you're looking from.
   But that means, I guess, I must accept that we'll reverse our roles,
   And you all say it's a better way, as this NEW LIFE unfolds.

Well then, when I drop my spoon or knife or fork, or spill my soup or drink,
Won't you please look back across the years...just stop, reflect, and think
   Of you there in your highchair, every time you came to eat,
   You spilled your food, on one or more, of floor, or chair, or feet...

Or on your clothes, or in your hair, some even up your nose;
You had your food all over you...and where else, only "goodness knows!"
   But that was fine, okay by me, that's part of life's little game,
   And I tried, HARD, to understand, so please...won't you do the same?

And when you repeat a thing to me, a half-dozen times or more;
Or when I stumble, or when I trip a bit, as I try to cross the floor;
   Can't you remember, years ago, those songs and nursery rhymes
   That I repeated o'er and o'er...I'll bet, some a thousand times;

And how you fell into my arms...as you tried to take each step?
But I was patient with you back then, and enjoyed just giving HELP.
   So, when my step is a little shaky, and I walk with two left feet,
   And my room isn't all that tidy...and my appearance not quite so neat;

Please remember, in your childhood, your slouchy style and frizzly hair,
And your room was usually in a mess with toys strewn everywhere.
   And I'll never forget that runny nose, and those dirty diapers, too...
   But it was all worthwhile away-back then because of LOVE for YOU!

And remember your very first birthday, your party was OH SO GRAND...
And the time you were so very sick, how I sat and held your hand?
   We prayed...and gave you medicine, and wiped your fevered brow;
   So, I guess, the TIME has finally come...to accept your HELP just now.

So, won't you please take a tiny moment from your busy schedule and see
How your patience, concern, and kindness means the "WORLD" and "ALL" to me!

TWO HEARTS

My daughter and son-in-law.

A brand new son, a little Lad,
His dad and mother named him Brad.
   As he looks back to those yesterdays,
   So many good times in so many ways;
All of the ball games, all of the fun,
Sometimes he lost; sometimes he won;
   But he gave it his all, his very best,
   And in everyone's heart he passed the test.
There was golfing and fishing and hunting, too,
In the evening hours or the morning dew;
   And when one day he met a special someone,
   He knew then his life had just begun.
And very soon they fell in love,
To each...God's gift from up above;
   Such carefree times, what joy, what bliss,
   And each remembers their very first kiss.
They looked ahead; they made their plans,
Their future in each other's hands;
   Their hopes were high, their future bright,
   Everything was good; their hearts were light.
And the day soon came and both could see
They were ready for a family,
   But as years raced on and time flew by
   Oft times they had to stop and cry.
Their best laid plans, their greatest hope,
Seemed to somehow vanish in clouds of smoke;
   All the hurt and disappointment is so hard to bear
   As their wants and hopes seem to drown in despair.
But someday, somewhere in another land
They'll feel the touch of GOD'S own hand,
   When their aching hearts have had time to heal
   And the gnawing pain they no longer feel,
Then someday, somewhere, they'll be able to see...
And then they'll know why it had to be.

221

WAITING FOR YOU
A Commitment for our Youth!

Somewhere I know
There is one who is true,
One who is waiting
For me to find you.

We're keeping our treasures
Both clean and free,
I'm waiting for you...
You're waiting for me.

The lure of life's pleasures,
The illusion of sin,
Keeps returning to haunt us
Again and again.

It's been quite a struggle,
Temptations every day,
But somehow we've managed
To keep it that way.

It's well worth the waiting
I want you to know,
And when we become weak
God's word helps us so.

It gives us direction,
It encourages and uplifts...
Two virtuous lives
Are the Ultimate gifts!

WILLIAM RALPH'S TREASURE

My daughter-in-law

What do you say…what do you do,
When you're out of money and flat broke, too?
Do you find a job? Do you go to work,
Or just lie around and be a jerk?

Well, I tried my hand at many a thing.
I didn't join a band or try to sing
But I worked for Locke and I worked for the State.
I liked it pretty good and never was late.

I coached football and taught some, too,
But those teenage kids they get to you,
So I tried something else, an Engineer,
And that's pretty good, it's now my career.

I do like to hunt and fish a lot
But what I want most I actually got;
I struck it rich. I'm wealthy now!
You want to know when? You want to know how?

God has put many riches in this old world;
Some find gold or silver or ivory or pearl.
Many get rich on oil or gas;
Well, I searched here and there and finally, alas;

I built me a house and own some land,
And I've got two kids that are really grand,
And I found a DIAMOND along the way...
And DIANNE is the DIAMOND, I'm happy to say!

WHY

What have you failed to do today
Just because you did not do...
Was it a little, tiny thing
Someone requested of you?

Your friend, your wife or daughter,
Your husband or your son,
They needed such a simple thing
You could, so easily, have done?

That small request they asked of you
That could have meant so much
Became a heartache...and a hurt...
Pain grasped them in its clutch.

Missed deeds can be a weapon, true,
That hurts and wounds the soul;
Why can't we feel how others feel?
Oh let this be our goal.

FRIENDS

A REAL FRIEND

I'm so glad you came to see me,
I've been thinking quite a bit,
Since I have grown so feeble
I just sit...and sit...and sit.

I think about the days when I
Was just a carefree kid,
I was a very active youth...
Can't believe some things I did.

I use to roam all through the woods
And hunt the birds and bees;
I loved to play among the rocks
And climb up great big trees.

On sunny, summer afternoons
I'd go down to the park,
Then jump into the muddy creek
And play 'till it was dark.

When I grew up things changed a bit,
I married the "love of my life"...
Oh, how I loved those precious days,
And especially my dear, darling wife!

You've been so good to talk to,
You always understand...
The way you sympathize with me,
And smile, and take my hand.

You're such a lovely person,
A real friend, I want to say,
Since you came by to see me
I can make it another day.

THIS BOWLEGS AFFAIR

Given at Bowlegs Alumni Banquet June 16, 2001

The years have come and the years have gone
But us old Bowlegs Bison are still rolling on.
   Every summer, in June, we come back each year
   And we're hoping the 'OLD GANG' will all be here.
Seventy years of schooling at "Old Bowlegs High"...
"And a "Million Memories!" came someone's reply.
   The trophy case is bulging from all the victories won;
   And those school trips and parties were so much fun.
My, my, how the time flies so swiftly away
But People and Memories make this ONE SPECIAL DAY!
   Each word and each smile is a path to the past.
   Don't you hope for many more...Don't you hope they last?
All the hugs and the kisses, and a few Sacred tears,
Make it even more SPECIAL as we keep counting the years.
   The world divides time by B.C. and A.D.
   But at Bowlegs we have a different way, you see.
A more correct division of time can be recorded as thus;
By the E.E. and E.R. era...now before you make a fuss...
   Let me explain why this is a much more correct way;
   Just look around at all of you people here today.
I'd bet my last dollar against your nickel and dime
That most of you here represent the E.E. era and time!
   Most things sure are a lot different for young folks today
   Than during the 'EMERSON ERA' ...that was our heyday!
How many attended Bowlegs during the E.E. time?
And now, 'AFTER EMERSON' era..., hey, that's no crime,
   But the A.E. era...that's a whole new "ball game'
   And there's very little about it that's exactly the same.
There's a very sobering question that now suddenly appears;
Where are all of those graduates from the last forty years?
   Do you think the A.E. Alumni will keep up this annual event,
   Or do you think it will vanish and they'll wonder where it went?
Will they miss this yearly excitement, this B.H.S. family affair?
It'll take a lot of 'doing' or it'll soon fade away in 'thin air'
   Do you think we are griping, or bragging, or telling it like it is?
   Well, give us the benefit of the doubt...come on...gee whiz!
I'll say just one more thing and then I'll sit down
And you can give me a smile, or give me a frown.
   I hope they'll meet, and relive, the good things of the past;
   And let me say, from my heart, I sincerely hope it will last!

GOING BACK

Given at Bowlegs Banquet in 1986 on my 40th graduation anniversary, and again in 2009.

I was driving along the highway, going back, the other day,
Back to where I spent my childhood, where I used to learn and play.
From Seminole I headed south, expecting soon to get a view,
Of familiar sights and places and meet an old friend or two.

But hey...I'm on the wrong road! No...the sign said straight ahead,
So I drove on down the new highway heading south, just like it said.
I should have expected something, but I tell you folks, you know...
It was really a big surprise to find there's no Maud "Y" and no Roscoe.

But soon I came upon a sign that said "BOWLEGS"...I drove just past
And turned on to a well worn street...I'm finally here, back home at last.
Now let me see...where is it now? Oh, it's not here anymore,
Not my old home, nor Joe's Cafe...not a single grocery store.

I did pass a Post Office building but that's about all I could see,
And nothing about it seemed the same like it used to look to me.
The old water tower had disappeared and in its place, one new...
There was hardly a thing that hadn't changed...maybe I'll find one or two.

"Is this really the place," I asked myself as I slowly drove on ahead,
And then I saw what I came to see and this is what it said;
"B -O-W-L-E-G-S,"...I remembered from years before...
"BEST LITTLE TOWN IN THE WHOLE U.S." Just what I was looking for!

And then I saw the old school house still standing where it stood,
Mr. Emerson's place, and the football field, and it made me feel mighty good.
I remembered the bus trips and parties, the pep squad and band that would play
At the half time of every ball game...and the hamburgers at the cafe.

I remembered those lovesick couples, and the one I was dying to date,
And the night I got into trouble when I came home a little too late.
I remembered one day on the campus the teachers were as mad as could be,
Someone had climbed the pole, took down the flag and they were trying to blame it on me.

Then I stepped in where we held our assemblies, where we pledged to our flag, unfurled,
I wondered where everyone is now...guess they're scattered all over the world.
I remembered receiving my Senior ring, my pictures, my cap, my gown...
And the very last time I walked down the isle, so slowly...and then I sat down.

Then I looked at the pictures in the "Hall of Fame" and my mind began to whirl...
So many thoughts raced through my mind of most every boy and girl.
How many of them are still living? Several were lost in the war,
And some of our mates and dearest friends have parted, and gone on before.

Yes, so many memories and most of them good, memories of things gone by...
Soon I felt a lump come in my throat...and I wiped a tear from my eye.
Then I asked whom I thought was a student, how High School was going these days,
"Sir, I've been teaching six years," she said, "And I have nothing but praise."

228

My...young people look so young these days, and I wanted to stay and talk,
But I was almost late for a special date so I walked on down the walk.
I looked and found the old highway, the one that I had known,
But it all seemed strange as I drove along...the oil camps and kids were all gone.

I then crossed the tracks into Seminole and dragged Main Street once more,
Gone were the bustling "Oil Boom" days, the busy people in every store.
When I finally arrived at the Banquet I wondered if this was the place...
"What are all of these old folks doing here?"... I thought as I looked at each face.

Just one person looked halfway familiar of the dozen I passed on my way,
But it has been a while since I saw the old gang, yes...many and many a day!
Is this actually nineteen-eighty-six, And the third week in June almost past...
The twenty-first day, and Saturday eve...I can't believe time passes so fast!

Well, I stopped at the table to register in and the lady gave me a look,
"Will you please give me your name?" she asked, "I want to write it down in my book."
"Bill," I replied. "Bill, who?" she asked; I glanced at the name on her dress...
"Well, Sarah Jane Snyder, don't you know me?" "Bill Swain...you were always a mess!"

Then I hurried to find my classmates, could it possibly have been forty years?
I wondered how different it now would be, would we laugh...or shed a few tears?
I got a few stares as I slipped through the crowd, and I finally found the right sign;
It said, "WELCOME CLASSMATES OF '46!"...now that made me feel real fine.

Then I turned my head and our eyes met, and I wondered, "Don't I know you?"
She looked kind of sheepish 'cause she didn't know me; we just stared for a second or two.
Then I glanced at her name and she saw mine, and she gave me a great big smile,
Then she hugged my neck and whispered, "Bill...it's been a long, long while."

"Come on over and meet the gang," she said as she led the way.
"We have all been thinking about you and hoping you'd make it today."
Then we introduced ourselves to each other. We were all "eyes" and "ears"...
We looked listened and laughed and talked and traveled back through the years.

Us guys were discussing our Senior trip but the girls started making a fuss,
So we promised not to tell on them if they wouldn't tell on us.
We recalled the time we went to see Billy Bowlegs' old Indian grave,
And the fun we had at the wiener roast at the Wildcat Hollow cave.

I met people from other classes, too, who were just as excited as we,
Trying to find all of their old friends and see everyone they could see.
I met husbands and wives I had never met and made a new friend or two;
I met many I was very anxious to see, and some I'd forgotten...that's true.

Remember that big football hero that charmed all the girls, I suppose,
He had taken on quite a different look, he couldn't even see his toes.
That spindly guy who was so bashful and shy, he's now handsome, rich and well known.
He hit it big in the business world and owns a company of his own.

A few other things aren't like I thought they would be, If I'm honest I'll have to tell you,
That even back in those "good old days" I made a misjudgment or two.
That sleek, slim "cutie" that I used to "eye"... is now as chubby as I've ever seen,
And the one I turned down...'cause her mother was fat...now looks like a "Beauty Queen!"

And that tough "macho" guy... he now has a wife that leads him around by the nose..
And some of those shy and skinny gals have blossomed out like a rose!
Now I'm proud to say I have traveled a bit, been to several parts of the world,
But very few places can show us a thing when it comes to a good-looking girl!

Yet, we all must admit that people do change, but I'll tell you a secret I was told...
If you'll come to the Alumni Banquet each year you will never, never grow old.
I don't think that will ever happen to me, growing childish and old, like they say...
But I did leave my toys on the living room floor...so when I got home I could play.

I'm sure that if all of our families were here they would think we had a "loose screw,"
Poking fun at ourselves, reliving the past...but I love it...how about you?
Well, I hope I have touched a few heartstrings and brought you a little cheer,
If the Good Lord is willing and the creeks don't rise I'll see you all back here NEXT YEAR!

FRIENDS LIKE YOU

Have you ever been where the bottom seemed
    So high above your head,
And you felt so blue and lonely
    You almost wished that you were dead...

And when you tried to help yourself
    You slipped another notch below;
You'd give your "life" to leave that place
    But there seemed no place to go...

And then a friend just "happened" by
    And brought a cheerful smile
And was attentive to your words,
    Just listening, all the while?

They touched you where you hurt the worst
    And shed a tear or two,
They shared a word about God's love,
    They prayed a prayer with you,

As your friend departed from your world
    Of loneliness and night,
There shined a ray of "sunshine"
    And you began to "see the light."

At last, your load was lifted,
    And your hopes refreshed, anew...
We thank THEE, LORD, for friends like this
    Whose life is a reflection of YOU!

45TH INVITATION

The long summer is over and ended,
Another Christmas is drawing near,
And I wish you the best of everything...
And a Happy, Happy New Year.
    But something else is fast approaching
    That we've waited for a long time to see;
    An extraordinary and grand celebration...
    It's our "45th Anniversary!"
Most of you have made plans for next summer
And set aside this June 15 date,
But to you who haven't made the arrangements,
It's never, never never, too late!
    Really now, we are all anticipating
    That you and everyone else will be there,
    So please make your best special effort!
    Don't you think that is only fair?
A "45th" comes only once in a lifetime,
And it sure would be a big crime
If someday we looked back with regrettings
Because we failed to make it this time.
    Betty W. is planning something SUPER,
    And you all know what Joyce can do,
    Ms Hospitality, with a special "H"
    Planning her own special thing for you.
We are looking and counting and expecting,
And depending on you this next June
To be a part of our "Grand Celebration"...
It'll be more fun than a Honeymoon...?...?...?
    We never threaten, intimidate nor bully,
    Our policy is to always behave
    But if you missed the last letter I sent you
    I'll repeat the advice that I gave;
Nail a note on your door and mark your calendar,
Put a ring in your nose if that'll do,
But plan ahead for this date, if you let it slip past
It will forever, FOREVER haunt you!..!...!

ONE SPECIAL DAY
Given at the Bowlegs Class of '46's **45th Banquet** in 1991

Well, it's great to be back with you again
And see all of your smiling faces,
And hear each voice...and talk...laugh,
And visit old familiar places.
   I love the surprises, the greetings, the hugs,
   The excitement, the expressions, the smiles;
   These moments together make it all worth while
   Though we've traveled hundreds or thousands of miles.
And to you who didn't graduate from Bowlegs High
But have come from all over the land,
We extend a warm welcome to you, tonight;
Please stand up and wave your hand.
   I've changed my mind some since "86"
   Remember that secret you were told,
   That if you'd come to the Alumni Banquet each year
   You would never, never grow old.
Some still swear it's true, that things haven't changed,
They feel as young as they used to be,
But I have a different opinion of them...
There's a few things even I can see.
   These folks just won't admit to the changes of time
   But I don't hold to their point of view,
   'Cause lately I've looked in the mirror...at me,
   And now I'm looking at you!
Tell me, do Blanche and Phil and Alene Capps
And John R. Crews fit this list...
And Doris...and Howard...and Gladys...and Pete...
Is there anyone else that we've missed?
   How you see yourself in light of the past
   May be something on which you connive,
   But can we have it both ways? I think we can
   When our Bowlegs Reunion comes alive!
We can joke, can't we, and make fun of ourselves
And not let it hurt us a bit,
And not get up tight when this subject comes up
And maybe through a "wall-eyed fit."

Sure, we live in the present, but return to the past
For this "ONE SPECIAL DAY" in each year
And draw forth from our treasure of memories
And recall, and relive things so dear.
A few years ago, in 1986
I came back to a gala affair;
It was my 40th Class Anniversary...
They said our "old gang" would be there.
   I was really surprised that so many turned out,
   And there were hundreds of alumni who came;
   I counted 33 of my classmates that year...
   But please don't ask me to tell you each name.
I believe Tom Gallaher was our V.P. that year,
And Bob Stockton was our president,
And there were too many "Pools" and "Woods" to count
At that 1986 Alumni event.
   I remember at the banquet that "Goober" and "Biff"
   Kept those ten-gallon hats on their head;
   They're sacred to them, like all Texans believe...
   I guess they wear them even to bed.
And those "Class of '46" anniversary "T" shirts
Were the neatest that I've ever seen
On Colleen, Okie Jo, Betty Jane,
Martha Catherine and Wandalene.
   And someone asked how to spell "HOSPITALITY"
   Like you hear about "way down south,"
   "J-O-Y-C-E"...Garland yelled!
   "Well I'll be...shut my mouth!"
And the wiener roast that Betty Lou gave
Is something I'll never forget,
And our trip to the school with Ms. Rich and our class
In my mind I can still see them yet.
   We visited the school grounds and class rooms,
   And strolled down the "Hall of Fame,"
   And saw the new buildings and baseball field,
   And the new gymnasium's name.
Yes, down through the years many things have changed,
Our auditorium is named "EMERSON" today,
And they honored Coach Brooks in the State Hall of Fame,
And Pete Duncan...I'm happy to say.

But for an Alumnus to drive all the way to Bowlegs
On the new highway, isn't fair,
  You'll miss all the places and sights that once were,
  And be past...before you know you are there.
On that last trip we made I didn't have time
To see all that I wanted to see,
So, I made plans this year to take enough time,
And it was worth it all to me.
  I revisited old places where memories never dim,
  Like the fields where I used to play,
  And those big oak trees by the swimming hole...
  They're still standing there, even today.
But as I drove down the roads where oil camps once stood
I got a funny feeling, for sure;
No more Carter, Atlantic, Continental nor Gulf,
I.R.A., Sinclair nor Pure.
  There was one other place I just had to see
  So I hurried along the way,
  And all the feelings I felt when I arrived at the site
  I find it very hard to convey.
To my surprise the old church was gone
And a new one stood in its place...
As many hallowed memories flooded my soul
I could feel my heart pound and race.
  It was in that old church I learned of the Lord,
  And there I married my wife,
  And the message when my grandparents were laid to rest
  At the ending of their life.
And I had a good friend whose body
Was not as straight and strong as mine,
But deep inside his feeble frame
Beat a heart that was strong and kind.
  And in that old church, many years ago,
  Back when I was only a kid,
  I'll never forget a certain day there
  Because of what he did.
It was on a warm, Sunday evening
As we were all gathered there
At that little country church in Bowlegs,
In a quiet, worship atmosphere;

235

His heart was touched by God's Spirit
  As the preacher spoke the word
  And Leo Pool crawled, upon his knees
  To accept Jesus as his Lord.
You know, time may erase some memories
But others grow more fond and dear...
And it's so great to recall and relive the past
With you who have come back this year.
  But there are certain memories for some of us folk
  In this hustle and bustle of life,
  That are tough to face, and hard to forget,
  In this world filled with trouble and strife.
And there are those who are with us no longer,
And others suffer hurt and pain,
But I pray the best will come you way
...Until we meet again!
  So, if the floods of life have o'er taken,
  And fierce storms rage in your soul,
  If you're tossed and torn and beaten,
  And you can't seem to reach your goal
Just keep faith...the sky will lighten,
God will spare us, like He said;
Look...I see His Blessed Rainbow
Shining, brightly, up ahead!

48th BANQUET
THIS IS THE DAY
This poem given in 1994, 1997, and 2007 at the BOWLEGS Alumni
Banquets

Well, it's that time of the year and this is the day
When we meet, once again, down BOWLEGS way,
And may I ask you a question as we sit in this place
And look at each other, face to face.

   Why do we set aside this Special Day each year,
   And descend on this place from far and near?
   Is there something magic about the third week in June;
   Is it the ocean tides, or the dark of the moon?

Does the law require that we come back each year?
No! Not at all...it's something far more dear!
If we don't came back will God send the plagues;
Is there something mystic about BOWLEGS?

   No! No! It's the people...and memories from days long ago;
   It's the good times and friendships with those that we know;
   It's renewed, old acquaintances from all over the land,
   With many hugs and kisses...and shakes of the hand.

We went through childhood, mid life and now old age has arrived
And one of the biggest surprises is that we have all survived;
And we're richer, by far, when our fellowship ends
Because we've been, once again, with so many old friends.

   Though the days have sped by and the years have rolled on
   Let's think back to some things that now are gone.
   And may I suggest as we're in this gathering here,
   We try to pick out some moment that we hold so dear;

And let's pay homage to these moments, and give respect
To the people and places on which we reflect...........
What would you give, just for tonight, to travel back once again
To a Special Time and Place with your very best friend?

   Would you take that trip...What would you do?
   I think perhaps I might have a ticket or...two
   For a nostalgic journey down memory lane;
   ...Would anyone here like to go there again?

Yes, It's true now that each year some slip away
But their many fond memories will always stay,
And in future years when, we too, will depart,
We'll hold a warm place in somebody's heart.

But for tonight let's rejoice in our festivities here
Amidst all the joys of laughter and shouts of cheer!
Does it seem only yesterday that you were a kid;
Can you still remember some of the things you did?

Can you remember the day that you first went to school;
Did your teacher teach you the "golden rule?"
And all of those lessons, especially those A B C's
Were so hard for me...but for others, a breeze;

And all of that reading, and writtin'...and 'rithmetic,
I'll tell you right now, studying made me sick.
But even the bad things now, mostly seem good
And I'd love to go back, even now, if I could.

And remember, girls, those early, awkward years
How those naughty boys would drive you to tears?
Well, maybe you cried...or perhaps, for some it was fun;
And that first fight you had...was it lost...or was it won?

And then came the days when things changed a bit,
The boys charmed your fancy, and dazzled you with wit.
Then the parties, and the thrill of that first High School date
Until you got into trouble for coming home late.

Yes, those times were great in the "good old days"
And we still cherish them now in so many ways;
And there were band trips, and assemblies, and very special friends;
Aren't you glad that those memories just never ends?

And the ball games, and teachers, and each one's favorite class
But...some of those tests...Hey, did we really pass?
My favorite subject was gym class...and I loved after school;
You can see that my mother didn't raise no fool!

Ah, but the world has changed since those carefree days
And our paths have led out into different ways.
We're doctors, and housewives, and business women and men;
Some have traveled the world and we love to hear where all you've been.

238

We've touched many lives, all have played their roles
In this human experience...and it still unfolds.
And no matter how we've tried to make the old things stay,
The inevitable changes have all come our way.

But today we pay tribute to those "bygone days;"
Yes, that time has passed on...but the memory stays
And, you know, there's not many places left, when it's all said and done,
Where so many Old BOWLEGS People can have so much fun!

And I think we're all here for a very worthy cause
So, why don't we all stand up and give ourselves applause?
Yes, we're gathered again as we've done in the past
Just to enjoy ourselves! Don't you hope it will last?

But in fifty years from now, or maybe thirty-five,
Do you think today's alumni will keep this group alive;
Or, is the world different today, and have our values changed;
Or, at least, do they seem to have been all rearranged?

Can you imagine, for one moment, your teacher being afraid
To read from the Bible... or of a prayer they prayed;
Of teaching values and virtues they learned from the book?
Hey, it's high-time some folks stopped and had themselves another look!

Yes, sad to say, times have changed, it's different today,
And you know, tomorrow we'll scatter and go our own way
But, however you feel, and whatever you've done
We wish you the BEST when your race is run!

And now, may the joy of these Moments, in your heart, long remain;
So...I bid you ADIEU...until we meet again

55TH Banquet
CLASS OF '46 SPECIAL INVITATION

Well hello, good folks, what do you say?
I'm looking forward to a very SPECIAL day
On Saturday, June 16, two thousand and one,
And I'll tell you right now, we'll have bushels of fun!

Us BOWLEGS Alumni will gather once more,
And I don't care how many times you've been here before,
This is the one time you must, POSITIVELY, be here
'Cause the "Class of '46 will celebrate our 55th year!

I know you'll want to come and see the "ole" gang
And your presence here will start it off with a bang!
You'll get lots of hugs and perhaps a "little" kiss;
It'll be something for SURE you won't want to MISS!

And on Friday the 15th, Joan, Betty and Joyce
Want EVERYONE here. Remember...you have no choice!
They're planning a 55th SPECIAL for Friday night
So, plan to pack up your car or schedule your flight.

This will be the only 55th, EVER, with your "ole" schoolmates
So, do whatever you must do to REMEMBER these dates.
Put a RING in your nose; hang this LETTER in the hall;
TATTOO them on your chest; write them in BLOOD on the wall.

Cancel EVERYTHING else that might get in the way
And we'll SEE YOU next June...Hey, what do YOU SAY?
You already have?   You've CIRCLED these dates;
You're making PLANS now, to meet your "ole" CLASSMATES!

Well, until we MEET next June, let me wish you the BEST
For this year and next and ALL of the REST;
So have a Happy Thanksgiving and Merry Christmas, too,
And in the meantime, please, let me HEAR from YOU!

This poem was given at the "Class of '46" 55th Reunion party in 2001 and at the Alumni Banquet in 2003.

note: Billy Bowlegs was the Seminole Indian Chief whom the US Government tried twice to defeat in Florida but failed each time. Finally, they agreed that if Billy would leave Florida they would give him and his followers land in the Indian Territory, which land became the Seminole Indian Nation, and at Statehood it became Seminole County, Oklahoma. After several members of the Bowlegs family were massacred in their home the location became known as Bowlegs, now known as Bowlegs, Oklahoma.

AN ODE TO BOWLEGS

I think Chief Billy Bowlegs would roll over in his grave
And supernaturally, mysteriously arise,
If all of the quaint happenings in Bowlegs
Could, suddenly, pass before his eyes.

Then maybe he'd shout, and give a war-whoop
And quickly turn around,
And close his eyes and fade away,
Back to his happy hunting ground.

You know, the wild buffalo (Bison), coyotes and Indians
Used to roam this very range,
Then the white man, oilman and outlaws came
And made a COLOSSAL change!

There was wilderness, prairies and rivers
And great wide open spaces,
But with the white man, oilman and land run
Us OKIE were off to the races.

Everywhere, overnight, on foot or in wagon,
And without much preparation or thought,
People rushed in like a big swarm of bees
And many of them were caught

Without means, or a house, or a room, or a pot...
Or even a place to sleep;
They trudged down the roads past shanties and tents
And, at times, the mud was knee deep.

Some rooms were shared by three people, not at once,
But in three eighth shifts a day;
But when there Positively isn't anything else
What are you going to say?

There were shacks, shotgun houses, a few oil camps,
Someone lived under every tree;
People flocked in from every "who knows where"...
Some, just to see what they could see.

There were dance halls, girls and gambler,
And some shotgun weddings, I'm told;
In those early days around this place
Chances were you wouldn't live to grow old.

There was booze, bootleggers and fighting,
And shootings and killings, they say,
And everything else the old "WILD WEST"
Had to offer, by night or by day.

Notorious dance halls were appropriately named:
"Bucket of Blood", "Dreamland"...and "White way."
And what happened inside the "Blue Moon" walls
I think I'd better not say.

Yes, in its early heyday BOWLEGS was mighty tough,
Some say it resembled HELL;
It had Spanish Black, scores of prostitutes...and Ruby Scott,
...And don't forget BIG NELL.

How many people made up this crowd?
I can't tell you, I'd just have to guess,
But BOWLEGS was known, in the early oils days
As the toughest town in the whole U.S.

There were thugs, prostitutes and decent people
Milling in, around, and about;
No paved roads, no laws, no churches, no schools,
So the people began to shout...

Then God looked down on this pitiful town
And said something like this, more or less,
"I have already chosen someone for you
To straighten out a lot of this mess".

So, to this wild and wooly little territory town
The Emerson family came...
And as long as we live, and even beyond,
History will record their name.

As the ones who brought efficient and orderly schooling,
And EDUCATION..."MAN ALIVE"...
To this now FAMOUS and HONORED school system,
U.N. DISTRICT Number 5.

Out of the turmoil, chaos and confusion
A "brand new" school district arose,
To become the BOWLEGS SCHOOL SYSTEM,
And it grows, and grows and grows.

It became the largest Union Graded School System
In the whole entire U.S.
Hey... let's all stand up and give a cheer
To B-O-W-L-E-G-S!!!

And though the student body enrollment
Has, nowadays hit the skids,
In one year the 1927 enrollment
Grew from 267 to 2200 kids.

It's been 57 years since my schoolmates and I
Have parted and gone our ways,
But I still have many school memories;
They were some of my happiest days.

243

Can you remember your best grade school buddy,
And your first "date" in Junior High,
And when you got caught playing "hooky"
You had to tell a "little white lie?"

And the friendships and parties and ball games;
Some of those memories touch our soul...
And how some of you spent half of Saturday night
In the balcony of the "SEMINOLE!"

And that first love affair that curled your hair
And drove you nearly insane...
And the way they dropped you for someone else;
I'll tell you...that felt INHUMANE!

And can you remember eating your school lunch
At the cafe ran by Violet and Claud?
What food we had, and the fun eating there...
Go ahead...it's alright if you want to applaud.

BOWLEGS saw Pretty Boy Floyd and all the Kimes,
And don't forget Clark Gable,
In 1929 they filmed the ending to "CIMARRON"
The Academy Award Winning Movie, that's no fable!

Mr. Richard Dix and Irene Dunn
Were the movie stars who came.
And at the time Clark Gable was here
He hadn't as yet gained fame.

Later on something Special was added,
A paved highway and a railroad track;
And when the war was over
We joyously welcomed our service men back.

But some hearts were broken by their losses
And, perhaps, some have never healed,
But we've honored one loss at the BOWLEGS school,
We now play football on "KELLY FIELD."

Yes, BOWLEGS is dear to many a heart;
Many have come...and many have gone,
And for others who have yet to come this way
I know a brand new day will dawn.

But this is a new and different world
And most of these things have changed,
And if we were back in school today
I'll bet many things would seem strange.

So, let's all give thanks to the 'GOOD OLE DAYS"
And every memory that we hold,
And let's all stay YOUNG and GOOD LOOKING...
And Never, NEVER grow OLD!

Now, may your walk be straight and steady,
And your path not all uphill,
And we'll see you ALL back here next year
If it is the GOOD LORD'S WILL!

EIGHTY YEARS AFTER 59th Class Reunion Banquet in 2005

Well, it's eighty years after and what do you say;
After the GREAT OIL BOOM came BOWLEGS' way?
Now in the beginning BOWLEGS wasn't much;
There were a few Indians, trappers, and farmers and such.

   But when the GREAT OIL BOOM came BOWLEGS way
   It was a different time...It was a different day!
   I know the young folks never experienced that time,
   And some of the others don't give a dime.

But I think it's good to relive those days of yore;
Some can't get enough, they want more and more.
What have you done since you arrived here today;
Have you looked around...Did you loose your way?

   Who did you see...What did you do;
   Did you go and visit an old place, or two?
   Did you drive down that road...Did you see that old place;
   Did it bring back memories...Did it make your heart race?

Did you take a few steps and stand where you once stood;
Did it touch your heartstrings...Did it make you feel good?
You must have cherished that moment, and captured that thrill;
It won't fade away. No, no it never will!

   I like to make a few visits and see what I can see;
   You know it'll never be the same, but that don't matter to me.
   I like to see all the guys and see all of the gals,
   And see my old friends and all of my pals.

Most have had a good life, or so to me it seems,
We've shared in our heartaches, we've shared in our dreams.
So, in spite of our troubles and our aches and pains,
When this day is over we can count all our gains.

   Yes, more gains than losses, more memories, more fun;
   We should all be more thankful when this day is done.
   Hey, we've had a lot of fun reliving the past,
   But sad for some...it could be their last.

So to all of us "old folks" in our "golden Years"
Lets all stand up (if you can) and give three cheers:
(B O W L E G S, B O W L E G S, B O W L E G S)

   Well, goodnight my friends, goodnight and goodbye...
   And whether you laugh or whether you cry...
   Have Faith...Have Courage...Have Hope...Never Fear...
   And next year will you help us celebrate our (class of 46') 60th year?

60th Class Reunion in 2006
MEMORIES OF GOLD

I don't know of another place in the world
Where more "old memories" come to mind,
Where you can just be yourself, and meet old friends
And just let yourself unwind.

Most, have this date in June reserved each year
For our Bowlegs Grand Celebration,
And for that date, and time, and place...
I think it's the best in God's creation.

You know, I was thinking today about times of the past,
About certain happenings through the years...
And suddenly my thoughts almost blew my mind
As two-thousand and six appears.

I wondered if my math was correct,
If my numbers were added up right,
And when I found they were, I almost passed out,
My thoughts and feelings were "frozen with fright!"

Hey man...I could hardly believe it's been sixty years,
Not since my birth...but since I walked down the isle,
With all of my classmates, and reached out my hand,
For my diploma, encouragement, and a smile.

I've tried to tell, often times, through the years
About my life and times of yore;
About my town, and school, events, and friends,
Yes...that's what good memories are for.

There may be a few scattered here and there
That don't measure up to "par"
But I'll tell you what, I have a million more
That really, REALLY are!

When you close your eyes and open up your heart
    And look back across the years...
    Don't you feel kind of "funny"...and thrilled with "awe"
    And sometimes shed a few tears?

Some people cry for sorrow, some for joy,
And sometimes maybe we aren't sure which;
And when we get those deep feelings about the past
It's really hard to "scratch that itch!"

    I guess it's true, it must be true,
    My sixtieth year is here,
    And when I total the years it's a sobering thought...
    I hope old age is something to revere.

It's been a pleasure, it's been a real joy
To relive those days of old;
My cup is full...it's running over
With MEMORIES worth more than GOLD!

    At all of our gatherings through the years
    I really have had a "ball,"
    But folks, I tell you, I must confess...
    I think this was the "BESTEST" of all!

Do you want to know why I feel this way,
Why every June I come back here?
Well, I'll tell you plainly, it's no secret, you know...
I have made "IT" another year!

OUR 65th
June 2011

Hey, class of '46, and friends, what do you say...
Can you believe how fast time slips away?
I hope the last 65 years have been good to you;
You've earned your keep, you've paid your due.

And in spite of the aches, in spite of the pain,
Time for another SPECIAL Celebration has come again.
You've packed up your bags and packed up your car,
Some have come from near and some from far.

A very sobering thought came to me the other day,
How there are some things that only come ONCE our way;
So, on this 17th of June and on this Friday night,
I know our 65th "CELEBRATION" will be quite a delight!

We've met at Betty Lou's many times before,
She can really "throw a party" with food and fun galore.
We've met other places, too, with some hugs and kissin'
And if you weren't there you don't know what you've been missin'!

We visited the school that meant so much in childhood
And the now barren places where homes and oil camps once stood.
We recall the good times and the friends that we had
And most of those memories make our hearts glad.

We remember some things that had slipped our mind,
Maybe a time or a place where a friend was so kind.
Or a word fitly spoken in a time of great need,
Or a helping hand...or a much welcomed deed.

You know, Memories are great, Oh I hope they will last,
They take us back in time with friends of the past.
Good Memories are precious, they're worth more than gold,
Especially when they bring happiness from days of old.

Some folks say "TIME" passes, but I'm not sure they're right,
...I was a resting and a thinking a little last night...
You know, this thing we call "TIME" hasn't gone anywhere,
But there's a lot of folks not here in there usual chair.

Time doesn't pass...we pass... time stands still.
That's not very good news to us who are "over the hill."
But, Hey, this 65th is very SPECIAL and there can be only ONE,
And we're honored with your presence, so let's have a little fun!

Let's "live it up" tonight, we don't know what tomorrow may bring,
Whatever we do...Whether we eat, talk or sing;
Let's make more Memories that we know will last
And some time in the future today's Memories will be the past.

And tomorrow night our Banquet will be something, too,
Especially if everyone there gets to see you.
And now let me say, "It's so good to see all of you tonight,
So let's make the most of our 65th and "do it up right!"

ONCE AGAIN

Would you believe after all of these years,
And of all of the places we've been,
And after all of the water that's run under the bridge
We'd wind up back here, Once Again?

   I'm so thankful for every Bowlegs Bison and friend
   Who come back each year, without fail,
   In spite of everything that stands in the way,
   Whether tornadoes, hot weather or hail.

Don't you feel good each year when you get back here
And see an old time or long lost friend,
And you tell your "tall tales" for half the night
And wish it would never end.

   It is truly amazing, a miracle, I guess,
   That we've all found a possible way
   To pack up our "duds" and hit the road
   And be back at this Banquet today.

Just think of all the places in the whole, wide world,
Where had you rather be now?
Hey, give me one guess and I'll bet I can guess,
...'Cause you made it back here...some how!

   I know some are not here who have been regular before
   And Oh, how we miss every one,
   But for all who are present let's "light up" the day
   With our talking and laughing and fun.

Let's make the most of each day while it is still day,
And when the night comes we'll honor the night…
But while we're together for this celebration
Let's do each and every thing "up right!"

252

It seems most of our lives have turned out for the best,
Perhaps several disappointments for some,
But let's all thank the Lord for good memories and dreams,
And for good memories and dreams yet to come.

You know, our dreams can be as precious as silver and gold,
Whether looking back or looking ahead;
And it seems many have lived their dreams...and more,
While some have taken other paths instead.

Say, don't you wish you could travel, if only for tonight,
Back to certain places, once again,
And experience the same feelings, emotions and joys?
Could I hear a "hearty A-men?"

Hey, let's do take a little journey down memory lane
And roll back the "pages of time"
And recall, in our memory, some blessed event
That was so thrilling, or reverent, or sublime.

Just think now, in your mind, away back across time,
...And suddenly, in an instant, you're back there;
Now, let's relive that moment, and glean the treasures
Of moments and memories so rare.

Remember that time, that place, that person, that friend;
We all have memories that fit this "bill."
And they are precious, even priceless...they're not for sale,
No, not now...and they never will!

Yes, we all have treasures...of memories, that is...
And we're rich if we have One True Friend!
But just look around and you'll see a great number
And they'll be there until the End!

Tell me, are Bowlegs people really a different "breed"
Or is it something else, more or less;
Like friendship, and loyalty, and interest, and concern,
And other attributes that we may posses?

...Like living for others, giving to others,
And helping straighten life's winding road,
Or lending a hand to a friend...or man,
And help lighten someone's heavy load.

I ask, "Is there anything better than friendship and friends
When you have something blessed to share,
Or when you're hurting and need a helping hand...
Than understanding, compassion and care?

Now, to all of you friends who are with us this year
I wish you many, many, many, many more:
But if you can't make it back, just wave goodbye,
And we'll meet you over on that "Golden Shore."

THE SEASONS

We travel from winter to springtime,
From spring, to summer and fall,
Then fall gives way to winter again
Before springtime will make its call.

Then, when the beauty of summer has ended
And bright colors have said their goodbye,
Brown leaves will cover the landscape
And gray clouds roll across the sky.

Storm clouds hang on the horizon,
Winter weather is about to start,
A cold, north wind is blowing
But I feel a warmth in my heart.

Another season is swiftly approaching
In this cycle of endless bliss;
We'll gather with friends and family,
A few handshakes, some hugs and a kiss.

I'm so thankful for each new season,
We're much richer when each one ends,
If there's any one thing that surpasses it all
It's the FRIENDSHIP of my dear friends!

TRUE FRIENDS

How many friends do you really have?
  I mean friends who are really true.
Who know everything about you,
  And know everything you do?

Who know when to speak, to keep silent,
  Who give encouragement, correction and love,
Whom you know seek direction and wisdom
  From the Heavenly Father above?

Who laugh with you when you are happy
  And, in sorrow, shed compassionate tears,
Who share in the triumphant moments
  And calm you in all of your fears?

Who walk with you in the deep valleys,
  Who have traveled along the same road,
Who climb with you over the mountains,
  Who shoulder a part of your load?

How many friends do you really have...
  A thousand...or more...you suppose?
Let's try counting them on your fingers,
  And counting them on you toes.

If you've counted a hundred...or fifty...or ten,
  Even five...or two...or one,
Whom you know is a friend...a friend to the end,
  You are a mighty...Rich...SOMEONE!

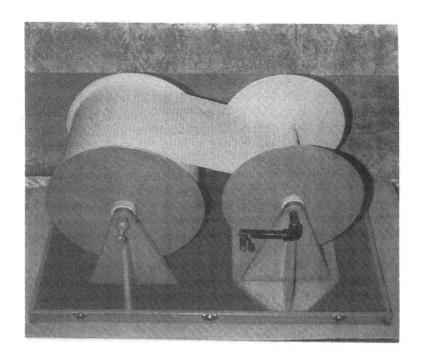

This scroll of the King James version of the HOLY BIBLE , including both Old and New testements, is believed to be the
only copy of the entire BIBLE ever written in its entirety on
one, continuous unspliced scroll. It was handscribed by
William O. Swain. The time required for writing covered a 33
months period from August 1977 to May 1980.

The overall measurement of this manuscript is 3,485 feet, unrolled it would stretch some 2/3 mile in length. It contains
109,824 lines of writing consisting of over 3/4 million words
and 3.5+ million letters. Placed end to end these lines would
reach 947,232 inches which equals about 14.95 miles in length.
This BIBLE weighs 50 pounds. It requires approximately 4 hours
to roll the scroll from beginning to end.

William "Bill" Swain

Made in the USA
Lexington, KY
29 October 2019